SDG Library

Bu
The complete guide to keep healthy and happy budgerigars

Copyright © 2018 Erika Busecan

All rights reserved.

ISBN-13:978-1987717563

ISBN-10:1987717562

Contents

Budgerigars or Parakeets — 5
- Description — 8
- Life span — 10
- Color mutations and varieties — 11
- Character — 23

The anatomy of a Budgie — 26
- External anatomy of a budgie — 26
- Internal anatomy of a budgie — 26

How to choose the right bird — 32
- General criteria — 32
- How to purchase a healthy bird — 34

Life with cage birds — 34
- Preparing your house for the new arrived parrot
- How to transport a pet bird — 35
- The "new arrived" parrot's diet — 37

The main diet of Budgies — 38

How to train your parrot — 49
- Understanding your budgie`s body language — 49
- Training and talking — 51
- How to potty train your bird — 57
- How to train parrots to stop biting — 58

Cages and accessories — 61
- Cage location — 61
- Cages — 62
- Toys and accessories — 66

Cleaning your budgie's "house" — 69

Disinfection with vinegar — 70
How to maintain your budgie's health — 71
Few advices about how to keep your budgies healthy — 71
The first sign of disease — 72
How to recognize the abnormal droppings — 73
Feather picking and self - mutilation — 74
Breeding — 75
How to setup the breeding cage — 78
Mating rituals — 78
Molting — 79
How to take care of the beak and the nails of your budgie — 81
How to clip your budgie's wings — 84
Bathing your parrot — 85
The special needs of the parrots — 87
Flying exercises — 87
Bedding materials — 88
The everyday life of a budgie — 89
Inappropriate perches — 90
First aid kit for your budgie — 90
How to hand feed a baby budgie — 93
Vitamins and minerals excess or deficiency — 96
Intoxication of the cage birds — 100
The most common diseases in budgerigars — 102
Foot abscess in birds — 103
Gout — 104

Enteritis (Inflammation of the intestines) 106
Obesity 107
Iodine deficiency or goiter 108
Psittacosis or parrot fever 110
Aspergillosis 111
External parasites **112**
    Lice infestations
    Scaly Face / Leg mite
    Dermanyssus gallinae
Internal parasites **114**
    Trichomoniasis or Canker 114
    Toxoplasmosis 115
    Tapeworms 116
    Threadworms or Capillaria 117
    Coccidiosis (Eimeria) 118
    Ascariasis 119
Skin and feather problems **120**
    Inflammation of the skin (Dermatitis) 120
    Xanthomas (Fatty tumors) 122
Reproductive problems **122**
    Excessive egg laying 122
    Egg binding 123
Aviary plants and shrubs **124**
Plants that can cause intoxication to your parrots **125**
Disclaimer **126**
More from the author **127**

<u>Budgerigars or Parakeets</u>

Budgerigars, scientifically known as Melopsittacus undulatus, belong to the Psittacidae family along with other parrot species like lorikeets, Eastern Rosellas, Indian Ringneck Parakeets, Quaker parakeets, Derbyan parakeets, Alexandrine parakeets and others. Wild Budgerigars are mainly seed eater birds and they can be found in semi-arid and arid places in Australia.

In the wild, they form large flocks in Australia's grasslands. During dry season these birds move over to wooded and coastal regions. These birds nickname is "budgie" and they are also known as parakeets, because of their long and flat tails.

The word "parakeet" refers to the most long-tailed parrot in the parrot family.

This is very interesting because there are many different types of parakeets and they come in different sizes and colors.

Indian Ringneck Parakeets for example, are very large birds in comparison with budgies and Alexandrine Parakeets are much bigger than Indian Ringneck Parakeets.

The Alexandrine Parakeets have the same tail shape as the other parakeets. Interestingly, Macaws have also long tails and almost the same characteristics as the smaller parakeets like budgerigar, rose-ringed parakeets, Eastern rosella, etc.... Considering these facts, macaws are not being recognized as parakeets. All parakeets are considered parrots, but large parrots like macaws are not considered parakeets. In my opinion the term "parakeet" should refer only to those parrots which have long and flat tail, regardless of their body size.

Bird breeders and ornithologist have different opinions whether parrot species are small enough to be considered "parakeets". This subject is quite confusing and should be debated further.

Budgies are also known as warbling grass parakeets, shell parakeets, parakeets, scallop parrots, zebra parrots, etc...

It is important to know that in the United States these birds are known as American parakeets or American budgies, while in United Kingdom breeders call them English budgies.

English budgies are bigger in size than the American parakeets, although both of them originates from Australia.

The English budgies were bred in England especially for pet trade and shows. English budgies are more domesticated birds in comparison to the American budgies.

In the wild they can be found in almost all parts of the Australian continent: New South Wales, South Australia, Queensland, North Western Australia, West and Central Australia.

These parrots were discovered on the Australian continent by the Europeans in 1789.

In 1840, John Gould, an English ornithologist, was the one who imported the first live budgerigars in England.

The native Australian people called these birds "Betcherrygah" or "Budgerygah". There are many translations of these words, like "good bird", "little bird", "good to eat", "tasty treat", "good food".

Other reports shows that the aboriginals followed these birds in order to find water and food plants. These people realised that the budgies could lead them to "good food" therefore, the name "Budgerigar" derives from the native Australian language.

Wild budgies are seed eater birds, so they need fresh water every day to survive. In their quests, explorers also followed budgies, because they knew they would lead them to water.

These birds are known to be capable of floating on the surface of water with open wings in order to drink.

The first captive successful breeding takes place in 1855 in Germany. The first recorded color variation was made in 1870, followed by a wide variety of color mutation shortly thereafter.

Wild budgies have been imported into France from Australia in 1890`s. Breeding budgies became a profitable business in many countries like France, Belgium, Holland and Germany.

In 1894, as budgies have become increasingly endangered, the Australian government banned the commercial export of these extraordinary birds.

Budgies became very popular in United States in 1920.

Description

Budgies are small, colorful birds with long, flat tails. The original wild coloration of Budgies are green and yellow with black bars on the wings, head and back.

In adults the lower cheek is tipped with violet - blue cheek patches and there are three black spots under throat called throat patches. The bill is olive - gray, the legs are bluish-gray and the tail is blue in color. As other parrot species, budgies also have zygodactyl toes, that means: two toes are facing forward and two toes are facing backward.

Males and females look alike, but the colour of the cere (the bare skin at the base of the beak), may differ seasonally.

The color of the cere is blue in males and pale brown in females. During breeding season the female`s cere becomes chocolate brown color. The male`s head is also larger than the female`s head.

In some color mutations, the youngsters present bar markings on the forehead that recede with age and the cere present pink or purplish-pink color. The youngster`s eyes have dark irises that gradually become gray with age.

Wild budgies in their native habitat of Australia are smaller than those living in captivity, measuring 18 cm (7 inches) in length.

In general, the American budgie measures about 7,5 inches (19 cm) in length, while the English budgie average between 8-9 inches (20.32-22.86) from the beak to the tip of the tail.

A budgie`s body weight is around 30-40 grams.

The English budgie has larger head, prominent chest and puffier feathers around their faces and crowns.

The budgerigars gender can be easily determined by their particular markings and behavior. The male`s head is larger and rounder, the cere is blue (but in some color mutations the cere could be purple to pink). The male is also more cheerful and very vocal in comparison with the female.

Life span

In captivity birds can live much longer than in the wild, with the condition that they get all the necessary nutrition and care which they need.

Even in captivity, the lack of food, incomplete diet and improper care of parrots could lead to a considerably shorter life span. American budgie`s average lifespan is up to 14-15 years.

Regretfully, the English budgie has relatively shorter life span, it lives only 6-8 years.

Color mutations and varieties

Color mutation refers to a bird who`s plumage presents a different color than we would normally find in the wild. Most colors have been established in captivity: light-green, dark-green, green-violet, yellow, violet, violet-blue, olive, grey, blue, albino, etc...

In Belgium the first color mutation was the yellow or yellow phantom in 1872, the blue in 1878 and in 1882 a yellow with red eyes.

In Danemark there is another color mutation, the yellow with green spots on the chest, on the back and black spots on the head and on the wings.

In stores, the most popular colors are blue, green and yellow. Males and females look alike, but the colour of the cere (the bare skin at the base of the beak), may differ seasonally.

Nowadays, Budgies come in an enormous range of *colors and varieties*. There are 32 primary color mutations that are split in two main types. One of them are white-based (Recessive) mutations like whites, grey and blues and the others are yellow-based (Dominant) mutations like yellows, greens and grey-greens. There are also hundreds of secondary color mutations and a multitude of color patterns and feather mutations.

The original or classic type of budgie is called Light Green Normal.

The most common varieties are: Greys, Lutino, Green, Yellow, White, Olive, Cobalt, Mauve, Albino, Clearwings, Greywings, Opalines, Fallows, Cinnamon, Violet, Yellow-faced Blue, Pied, Spangles, Lacewings, etc...

Light - Green Spangle

Dominant - Pied Cobalt

Pied Opaline Sky-blue Recessive

Yellow-face Cobalt

Skyblue Normal

Greywing Light - Green

Cobalt Opaline

Yellow - based Spangle

Wild-type Green

Black - eyed White with sky-blue belly

Character

These beautiful, small sized birds are the most popular pets in the world. Budgies are very affectionate and cute birds and usually friendly and some of them are easy to tame.

They can mimic human speech but they are not as good as the larger parrots: (African Grey parrots, Cockatoos, Macaws, Amazon parrots, etc...).

Not all budgies are capable to talk and this mostly depends on how much time the owners are spending with their birds. You have to dedicate at least 1 hour daily to your bird to make it tame and therefore to teach him/her to talk. A hand - fed bird (especially a young bird) is likely to learn to mimic human speech much easier than an untamed bird.

So if you decide to bring a budgie as a pet in your house, you'll have to know that you will need to dedicate time, patience and affection, every single day to your bird.

A well-trained budgie can be a delightful companion, but some of them could be stubborn and mischief birds.

Budgies are quiet birds in comparison with other parrot species and they are non-destructive by nature. *Some people may consider these birds as loud as the other parrot species, if they are not used with the parrot's vocalization. If you have never owned cage birds, than you probably will consider the budgies loud birds as well.*

A single bird is likely to be quieter than one that has another bird to interact with.

Their entertaining and gentile character makes them suitable for most people and they are capable to love the entire family members.

Budgies are very playful, active birds, in fact they have good imitating and acrobatic skills.

The American parakeet or budgie is more active than the English budgie and they are not as time demanding as larger parrots.

A tamed budgie love to chew on your hair, hide in your pocket, or even fall asleep on your shoulder.

Some people (people who have never owned a pet bird) think that their budgie will bite them. The bird won't bite you as long as you try to manipulate the bird by using your hands and fingers in a friendly and calm way.

The beginner pet bird owners use to react when their bird wants to step up on their finger by grabbing the finger with their beak, therefore they think that the bird is going to bite and the frightened owners pull their fingers away. What the bird really wants, is to step up on your finger, because s/he thinks it's a branch of a tree. If you pull your finger away, it's going to grab and hold your finger with its beak.

In fact, you will reinforce the bird for another bad habit and s/he will realise, that grabbing your finger, will cause another reaction, another drama. Therefore, you have to use positive reinforcement for behavior not resulting in biting.

Youngsters should be socialised to many people and exposed to a variety of situations such as handling by friends, visits to the veterinarian, nail and wing clipping (if necessary), to avoid fear of new situations.

The anatomy of a Budgie

External anatomy of a Budgie

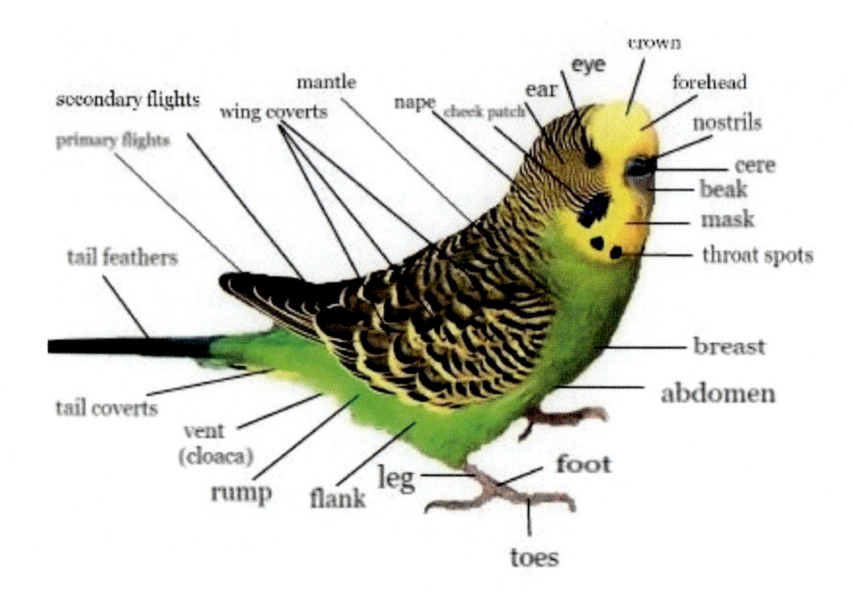

(Diagram of a budgie with labels: crown, eye, ear, forehead, nostrils, cere, beak, mask, throat spots, breast, abdomen, foot, toes, leg, flank, rump, vent (cloaca), tail coverts, tail feathers, primary flights, secondary flights, wing coverts, mantle, nape, cheek patch)

Internal anatomy of a Budgie

The bird's body is covered with feathers, which helps maintain body temperature during the flight. The feathers are made out from keratin, the same protein found in our hair and nails. The feathers are covered with a thin layer of grease and feather powder. The grease is extracted with the help of the beak from the uropygial gland, preening gland or oil gland and distributed on the feathers. The uropygial gland is located at the rump or the lower back of the bird.

At some birds, like pigeons and some species of parrots, the uropygial gland is missing or is not properly developed and they have feather powder.

Hyacinth Macaws and Amazon parrots do not have uropygial gland.

A plumage which is permanently protected with grease or feather powder can`t become wet, because the rain will just simply flow down from it.

There are several types of feathers:

Contour feathers cover most of the surface of the bird and they protect the bird from sun, rain, wind and injury.

Flight feathers are the large feathers of the wing and tail. The tail feathers act as brakes, controlling the orientation of the flight. The flight feathers basis are covered with smaller contour feathers called coverts. There are several layers of coverts on the wings.

Down feathers are soft, fluffy and small feathers and can be found under the contour feathers.

Filoplumes are very fine, hair - like feathers.

Semiplumes provide aerodynamics, form and insulation.

Bristle feathers are usually found on the head.

The skeleton of the bird is adapted to flight function, so the bones are hollow and lightweight, without marrow inside.

In some bones, the hollow cavities contain extension of the air sacs from the lungs, which helps the bird to get the oxygen it needs to fly easily and quickly.

The beak has no teeth, it`s also known as bill and it has two parts: the upper mandible and the lower mandible.

The upper mandible does not move independently from the skull and the lower mandible can move independently.

The wings of the bird are much like the arms and hands of the humans.

The most important muscles are the breast muscles and those of the wings.

The breast muscles represent one third from the total body weight of the bird and they are attached to a large bone, called the keel. The keel extends from the breastbone (sternum) down along the chest and stomach.

Respiratory organs

Birds have a single nasal cavity and the larynx does not have vocal cords, it helps only to lock trachea during swallowing.

They have lungs and they have also nine air sacs through which air circulates. These air sacs allow a continuous flow of air through the respiratory system.

Digestive components

The beak or bill serves for eating, preening, communicating and other abilities.

The crop is the muscular pouch and it can be found at the end of the esophagus and serves as a chamber for storing and softening food, until the food already in the stomach moves on through the rest of the digestive system.

The crop leads to a two - chambered stomach: one called *proventriculus*, which has the role to produce stomach enzymes for breaking food down, and the other chamber called *ventriculus* or *gizzard*, a powerful muscular organ, which takes the place of teeth and here the seeds and an assortment of grains of sand are squeezed until the seeds break up into a digestible form.

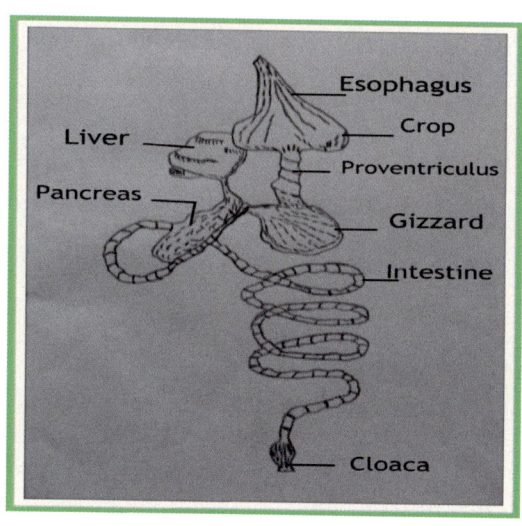

From here, the food goes through thin then thick intestine and the digested food arrives in cloaca. The cloaca is the final part of a digestive tract and it is a small chamber with a mucous membrane. Parrots excrete their feces and their urine from the cloaca and it also plays an important role in reproduction.

Urinary tract organs

The kidneys of the bird are located on both sides of the backbone and they are protected by the air sacs. The urine will be eliminated through the cloaca and it can be a soft or solid substance and it contains uric acid which makes it very corrosive.

Genital organs

Cocks have testicles and females have ovaries inside the body and when the birds are ready to breed, their reproductive organs (testes and ova) swell and produce the sperm and ova. At cocks the sperm is stored in the cloaca, until an opportunity to mate arises, and hens will receive the sperm into their cloaca before it will fertilize their ova.

Females have only one ovary and one oviduct, but in early stages of embryonic development each female bird has two ovaries and only the left ovary develops into a functional organ. During the breeding season the size of the ovary is changing, becoming larger. Males have paired abdominal testes which can be found inside of the cavity of the body. During breeding season the testes increase in size, becoming almost five times bigger than the initial size.

Body temperature is between 104 - 105.8 degrees Fahrenheit (40-41 degrees Celsius), which increase with 32.9 degrees Fahrenheit(0.5 degrees Celsius) during sexual maturity, during egg laying process and in molting period.

The eyes

Most of the birds have their eyes placed on each side of the head. With the help of their mobile neck, the bird can see the surroundings in a radius of 360 degrees and can fly away rapidly if there is any danger nearby. The lower eyelid of the bird is mobile and the upper one is almost fix. The third eyelid which is called nictitating membrane is hinged at the inner side of the eye and it serves to protect the eyes from bright light, wind, etc...

The ears

The ears are tiny, round holes situated in the right and left side of the head, behind the eyes and they are covered with feathers. There are no cartilaginous pavilions, but inside the ear there is the organ of balance. When the bird suffer from ear diseases, the organ of balance is also affected. The sick bird can't hold itself properly on the perches and its head is twisting to the affected ear.

How to choose the right bird

General criteria

Budgies are very lovely exotic birds, so if you want to be happy with your bird, you have to study your parrot species personality and abilities, which will help to create a perfect pet-owner relationship, leading to a happy life together.

Before you decide to purchase a bird, you have to be aware of the fact that very few birds could match your expectations and you have to realise that these birds will be your companions for many years.

Don't forget that your bird will need food, cage cleaning and at least once a day fresh water.

Your budgie needs your companionship and affection and it's very important to spend few moments daily with it.

If you are uncertain about keeping a pair or just a single budgie, then you have to take into consideration that a single bird is much easier to maintain and to train. But if you don't have enough time to spend with your bird every single day, then I would strongly recommend to buy a pair of budgies instead of a single bird.

If you decide to purchase a single bird, but you are uncertain about the bird's gender, then you have to take into consideration that the males are ideal pet birds and can be easier domesticated than females.

What I try to explain is that males are more friendly and more calm than females are. This does not mean that people should avoid caring for females. A young female or a well trained female budgie could be a very good companion for you as well.

Budgies have a very sweet personality as well. Males are not as noisy and destructive as females during breeding period and they can learn much easier to speak, because of their capacity for imitation.

Budgies should not be allowed unsupervised freedom in the house, because they can easily ingest harmful household toxins or dangerous items.

Another personal advice: take the bird with you if you are going in holiday, because they just love going in holiday and love spend all their time with you and your family.

How to purchase a healthy bird

Purchasing a birds directly from the breeder or from the pet store has multiple advantages. You can get information about their health condition, their provenience and also you can check the quality of the environment where they've been kept. You have to know a few aspects which could indicate hidden diseases: the bird has to be active with a good stability on its feet; the nostrils must be clean without secretion; the feathers around the beak must be clean; the bird's breathing has to be clear without whistling sounds; the eyes have to be clear; the missing feathers from the wings or tail could indicate "french moulting" (viral disease which leads to feathers loss); dirty feathers (with feces) at the vent area could indicate digestive system problems.

Life with cage birds

Preparing your house for the new arrived parrot

Before you bring your beloved bird in your house, the first thing you will have to do is to find a proper place for it. This place has to be quiet and without any air currents.

The cage has to be equipped with all the necessary things: food, water and toys.

First day it's better to offer a little bit of privacy to the new arrived bird. Even if some people, especially kids like to watch these beautiful birds, it is highly recommended to cover the cage, especially during the day.

If you already own birds, the new arrived bird has to be isolated in a separate cage. You have to leave the bird to get used with the new conditions and with you, the new owner. A parrot is considered accommodate when it does not get scared at the appearance of the owner and when it is feeding properly. (A frightened parrot freeze in place, hold its wings tightly against its body and flatten its feathers.)

After the accommodation process, if you want to move your bird in other cage with the other birds, instead of stressing the bird by catching it with your hands, you better bring closer the entrances of the two cages and leave them in this position for a while. You have to give your bird the time to adapt slowly and to get into the other cage when she/he is totally relaxed.

How to transport a pet bird

Transportation of the birds can be dangerous when it's done improperly and may cause serious problems to your bird.

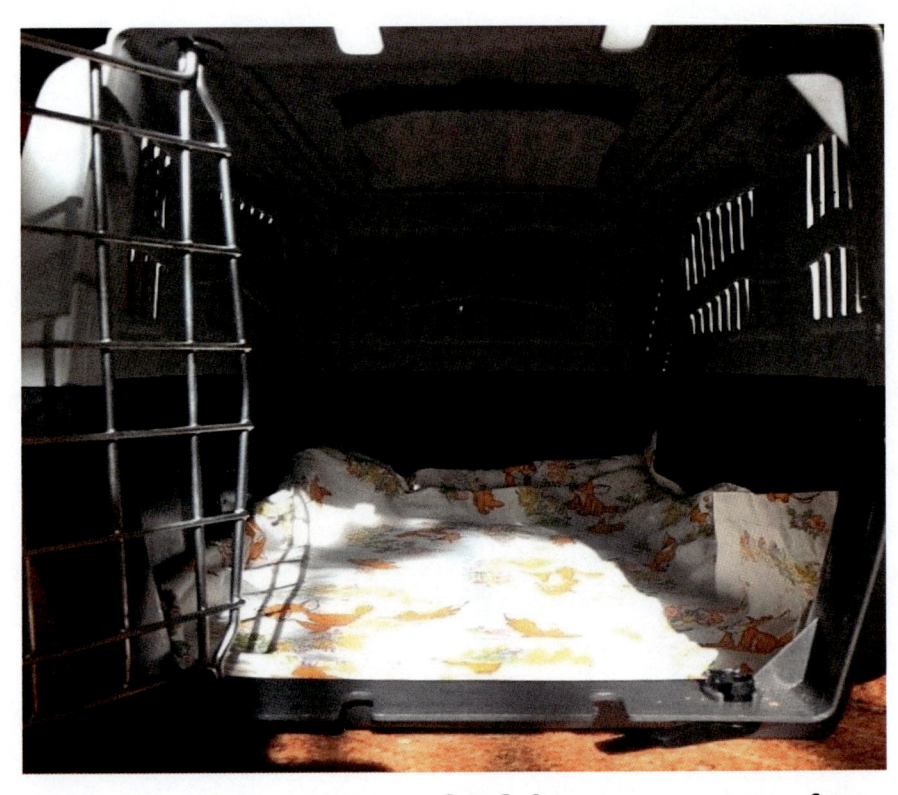

When you transport your bird from your vet or from pet shop to your home it is recommended to keep it in a special cage (carrier) without water and food bowls, and toys in it or in special bird carrier cardboard boxes with tiny holes in them for the bird to be able to breath and to avoid accidents.

If you choose the cage, you better cover it with a piece of thin, dark colored material and make sure that it has a hole on the top for the holder of the cage.

You can also transport your bird in a bigger shoe box (cardboard box) with lid. The box must present on the sides little holes (you can make them by your own with a larger nail), which are necessary for the air circulation inside the box.

The "new arrived" parrot's diet

When you purchase your bird, you have to know all about your bird's diet: what kind of food s/he has previously consumed. If the bird has not received the proper diet, then you have to replace it gradually. You'll have to offer your new arrived bird, freshwater and pieces of apple.

If your bird presents signs of weakness, you'll have to offer some moist biscuits (soaked in water, herbal tea or milk) and egg paste.

 If s/he looks healthy, you can give your bird the usual food, but also you can add in his/her food some poppy seeds (poppy seeds will have a calming effect on your bird`s health).

The chamomile tea (instead of water) has also a good calming effect and makes your bird to feel more relaxed.

The main diet of Budgies

In the wild budgies eat a great variety of grass seeds, berries, fruits, vegetation and insects.

The main diet of our domesticated budgies should consist in high quality mixture of seeds and grains, fresh fruits and veggies, greens, nuts, a cuttlefish bone, grit and a mineral block.

Some breeders recommend the pellet food in addition, but in my opinion the traditional "seed mix - fruits, veggies, greens, nuts, grit and a mineral block to nibble", imitates these birds wild diet better than anything else.

When you buy ready-made seed mix, it's important to know where the different types of seed mix came from. Go online, search bird forums, ask around or speak with budgie breeders to find a good quality seed source.

Budgies mixture of seeds and grains consists of: barley, amaranth, millet, oats, canary seeds, buckwheat, corn, hemp, quinoa, rye, sweet corn kernels, wheat.

Budgies also love oilseeds, but these seeds should be offered in proportion of 10% from their daily intake.

Hemp, millet, rape and niger are considered grains, but I include them in the following list along with the oily seeds, because of their high fat content.

- *Rapeseeds*
- *Hemp*
- *Niger*
- *Millet*
- *Poppy*
- *Sesame*
- *Pumpkin*
- *Rapeseeds*
- *Sunflower*

Seeds have to be fresh, free of dust or mould and should never be roasted.

Budgies are very likely to gain weight, so owners should monitor their fat intake. Overfeeding leads to selective feeding and wasteful throwing of food.

A picky budgie will choose the fattest seeds, because they are tastier and so the healthiest seeds are left behind.

Make sure that your bird is eating almost any type of seed from the feeding bowl. If not, you should limit the quantity of the food. In the first hours of the morning, offer your bird only two teaspoon of seeds (two teaspoon per bird) and do the same thing during evening and observe your bird`s behavior.

I am sure that s/he will learn to adapt and after a few days your budgie will eat any type of seed from the feeding bowl and not just the tastiest.

Cereals like wheat contain high level of sulphur, which can be administered to your parrot as a food supplement in molting period. The sulph helps to regenerate the plumage of the bird, that's why you need to increase the quantity of wheat in your parrot's diet during molting period.

Oat seeds contain carbohydrates and a high level of albumins, which have an important role in development of young birds. Oat seeds are good choice for young budgies.

Adult budgies should have only 10% of supplementation in their diet from this cereal. Too much oat can lead to obesity in adult birds.

Corn seeds contain low level of vitamins and albumins, but they are very rich in carbohydrates. Budgies love to eat boiled corn, you can offer them as treats.

Bird owners usually offer their birds millet seeds as treat. Be careful with millet seeds, because too much of these seeds offered as treat could lead to obesity.

Place some seeds and grains on a container and soak them in water. Spray the seeds and grains with water to make sure they are moist. The seeds should sprout in about 5 days. Wash them before you give them to your birds.

Mix together all of the sprouted seeds, grains and legumes with the usual seed mix in one dish. A half a cup of this mix is enough for a day period. Sprouted seeds and grains provide nutrient-rich food, they are lower in fat and will help balance your parrot's diet.

If the weather is too cold for sprouting, the seeds and grains can be boiled about 30 minutes instead of sprouting them.

Sprouted seeds and grains are also good in weaning period for youngsters, because the softened shell is easier to break and the young birds can get used with the texture of seeds.

Beans, peas and lentils are considered legumes. The whole (not split) sprouted beans, peas and lentils should make up around 15% of the bird's seed mix.

The following is a list of the most commonly used legumes in the budgies seed mix:

- *Mung beans*
- *Adzuki beans*
- *Yellow peas*
- *Green peas*
- *Black-eyed peas*
- *Chickpeas (Garbanzo)*
- *Lentils*

You can mix some cooked white or brown rice with chopped broccoli, kale, spinach, peppers, dandelion leaves, and with cooked sweet potatoes. Your budgie will enjoy this tasty meal for sure.

The key to seed diet is variety. Offer your feathered friend high quality mixture of seeds, fresh fruits and veggies, nuts, greens, cuttlefish bone, grit and a mineral block. In this case you don't need pellets.

If you don't have enough time to offer your bird a fresh diet variety every day or s/he is a picky eater and you choose to feed your bird mostly with good quality pellets, you still need to provide fresh drinking water, fruits, veggies, greens, grit and a mineral block.

Pellet food for birds is a comparatively new concept that has gained popularity over the years.

Pellets are blend of vegetables, fruits, grains, seeds, and protein. They also include a variety of vitamins, minerals and nutrients that your bird needs. They are baked and then formed into shapes and sizes for different species. You should always check the package for feeding instructions on pellets. The smaller your bird, the smaller the pellets should be.

Some marketing agents try to convince bird owners that pellets are the perfect solution for them, because these products provide a balanced diet. However, if your budgies are used with seeds, it can be difficult to convert them to a pelleted diet. Even though, some budgies may find pellets tasty, if they are fed on them from an early age.

Pellets are often the most complete food you will be able to offer your picky eater bird. This way s/he will not be able to select the tastiest seeds.

Also keep in mind that some budgies never get used with the pellet food. All you can do is to teach your bird to get used with the healthy seeds and to offer him healthy greens or herbs daily. By giving your bird greens/herbs before meal, will increase its appetite and as a result, your bird will eat the daily portion of seeds with such a pleasure.

Vegetables are very good nutrients for your bird. Frozen veggies are just as nutritious as fresh veggies, so they are fine for your birds, just make sure that you read the label and avoid brands with added salt.

During summer you can offer them fresh veggies: cucumbers, tomatoes, broccoli, carrots, carrot greens, cauliflower, beetroot, green beans, pod peas, lettuce, peppers, celery, kale, asparagus, chopped Brussels sprouts, spinach, squash, sweet potatoes, sweet corn, spring greens, cress, endive, fennel, parsnip, pumpkin, mustard greens, parsley, radish, etc...

You can also offer your bird a variety of healthy fruits: grapes, melon, banana, pears, apricot, nectarines, papayas, guava, kiwi, mango, raspberries, strawberries, blueberries, blackberries, cranberries, grapefruit, oranges, cherries, oranges, papaya, plum, peach, pineapple, passion fruit, etc...

Calcium deficiency is common in captive parrots, especially in birds who may have been fed only on seeds and because of the lack of the natural sunlight. Try to expose your bird to natural sunlight as much as possible and you must provide a calcium rich diet for your bird, daily. Calcium is essential for healthy bones, muscle contraction and blood clotting, nerve and heart function. You can offer them calcium - rich vegetables and fruits like broccoli, carrots, spinach, dandelion greens, mustard greens, figs, kale, endive, apricots.

Budgies prefer to eat fresh herbs like:
- dandelion (Taraxacum officinale)
- white clover (Trifolium repens) – flowers and seeds yarrow (Achillea millefolium)
- ribwort (Plantago lanceolata)- leaves and seeds coltsfoot (Tussilago farfara)
- Chickweed (Stellaria media) – the whole plant and the seeds
- basil (Ocimum basilicum)
- shepherd's purse (Capsella bursa pastoris)
- chickweed (Stellaria media) – the whole plant and the seeds
- Marjoram (Origanum majorana); etc...

Basil (Ocimum basilicum)

Leaves and branches of fruit trees, oak trees, beech trees (Fagus sylvatica), willow trees (Salix alba) are the best source of vitamins so you can provide them directly from forests. You also have to offer the opportunity to your parrot to chew these kind of branches.

Offer your bird once or twice per week boiled eggs. Boiled egg shells are the best source of calcium, so you can offer them to your bird in crushed form.

Never give up when you try to offer your bird new foods and s/he refuses them. You'll have to try more than once, by mixing the new food into other foods. Birds learn through observation and they like to watch what we eat, so they will try the new food.

Uneaten food should be removed from the cages after two hours.

Avoid giving your bird avocado, chocolate, caffeine, sugary or salty snacks, milk products and alcohol!

Next, I will present 2 parrot mash recipes.

You will need: 1 cup of beans, 2 cups of grains, 2-3 carrots, 1 yellow, 1 red, 1 orange pepper, 1 cauliflower, 1 broccoli, dark green leafy vegetables (dark green lettuces, cabbage, kale, Italian parsley, broccoli green leaves, spinach, dandelion leaves, etc...), 2 apples, a half melon, 1 banana, 6 strawberries.

Separately soak grains and beans for about 6 hours each. Rinse each and add purified water (don't use tap water) until the beans and grains are slightly covered. Both beans and grains will soak up water, so be sure to cover them with extra water. During soaking, the beans will double in size and grains swell slightly. Boil for 15 minutes uncovered, then cover and simmer for another 15 minutes. Let cool and mix beans and grains together.

Mix together the chopped vegetables and dark leafy greens with the food processor and add some water.

Then mix together the chopped apples (avoid seeds), melon, banana, strawberries.

Combine equal parts of vegetable-green mix with bean-grain mix and then add 1 cup of fruit mix for each 6 cups of the above. Mix together and then put in freezer safe containers and freeze. Thaw for 24 hours in refrigerator before use. Do not use a microwave to thaw.

<u>For the second recipe you will need:</u>
brown rice and millet
sweet potato, broccoli,cauliflower, carrot, red pepper
beans
fresh parsley
2 slices of garlic
Cook the beans, brown rice, millet, sweet potato until they are ready.
In a food processor, grind veggies and beans into tiny little pieces.
Once the brown rice and the millet have cooled down, mix them in veggies.
Add the chopped garlic and the parsley.
Serve warm.

How to train your parrot

Understanding your budgie`s body language
Parrots usually show us how they're feeling and what they're going to do, by using their bodies in different ways, because they tend to communicate with us this way.
When they have their tail flared it means that they are excited or they will bite you. If your parrot has all its

feathers sticking out, with its wings held out from the body, then s/he could be ready to fight.

You can also observe a few clues at your parrot, when s/he intend to bite. It will open its beak and will spread its legs apart for a firmer grip on the perch. You can interact with your parrot to prevent the bite, when you observe these kind of signs.

When your parrot is happy to see you, a friend of yours or another bird, then s/he might puff out all its feathers or wag its tail or moves its beak up and down.

Another sign that shows your bird is happy, is when

s/he is stretching its body parts. For example, when the bird extends one wing and one leg on the same side of the body or it stretches its wings up or out.

When the black center of the eye (the pupil) is suddenly made smaller it might be a sign that the bird intends to bite, to court or to talk.

There is a trick that parrots play on some people by giving outward signs of friendliness and then bite when they are approached with fingers. These birds are doing such tricks to amuse themselves.

Training and talking

Budgies are easy to train especially on early stages of their life.

If a bird is left alone for too long, it may become indifferent and even scared in presence of humans. Therefore, it would be advisable for the owners to talk with their birds as much as possible and at least once per week free flight is recommended.

They are very intelligent birds, they need toys and a very strong relationship with humans to prevent behavioral problems and to attain best training skills.

If you really want to teach your parrot to talk, then you'll have to be more patient. You'll have to speak very often with him/her, and your voice has to be very calm.

If you want to teach a *young budgie* to talk, first of all

you will have to separate it from the others. If the youngster hears the other`s chirping sounds, then it will be difficult for him/her to imitate the human voice. Avoid sudden movements and put your hand inside the cage. Touch the bird and rub the head and ear area as gently as possible. Few days later, you can manage the bird to step up o your finger. Every time you interact with the bird, say its name.

On the first days, the bird will probably be scared and will fly away from your finger and will land on the curtain or on different objects in the room. Leave the bird to calm down and wait until the bird is flying back to you. Young birds usually fly back to their owners. If not, gently catch the bird and put it on your finger or place it back in the cage.

Continue to leave your bird out every morning, until it gets tamed. You will observe that your young budgie will fly on your shoulder, on your head or will chew on your hair. Repeat the bird's name and use the same tone, so s/he gets used to the word. Make sure that s/he is watching you when you are speaking. When the bird starts saying his own name, praise him.

The training lessons have to represent positive experiences for your parrots and they have to last for about 5-10 minutes, once or twice a day. Teaching your budgie to speak can take days, weeks or even months.

You can achieve very good result if you register the bird's voice and replay it. The bird will be very enthusiastic to hear his own voice and will learn to speak faster. You can even play videos with other budgies that are able to talk.

If you want to teach an *untamed/ new bird* to talk, then you will have to do it in a repetitive way. It is very important to have eye contact with your bird, when you are teaching it. You will observe that your bird will watch your mouth as well when you talk. When you say a word say it slowly and then repeat it for 5 times.

For example, every time you enter in the room, say "hello" to your bird. The bird will be very happy to see you return home and of course the word that will hear and remember will be "hello". The bird will associate you with the word "hello", because this is the more frequent word that you use when you enter in the room.

You have to combine training time with play time. You actually want to make the bird to enjoy the training, because s/he deals with a positive experience. You'll have to encourage your bird with the right words like "well done" and you'll have to offer rewards every time s/he will say the words right.

Your beloved budgie will mimic your laugh and will call your dog`s name.

The most common sign in parrots that shows that they are cooperative, is when they fluff up their feathers on their crests.

Be aware, never yell or hurt your parrot when s/he doing something wrong or you feel that s/he is stressing you. The bird will lose its confidence in you and will be very hard for you to regain it again.

When you feed your bird apples, you will have to repeat the word "apple" for at least 5 times. It is very important to let your bird to see that you love to eat apples. After every swallow that you make repeat the word "apple". You can even ask the bird if s/he likes the apple. When your budgie gets the delicious "apple", which is consumed with pleasure by yourself, your bird will associate the apple (food) with the sounds that you make or the word that you speak when you give it to her/him.

In case that you want to train an *untamed bird*, for the first days, don't try to handle the bird, because the most important thing is to get used with each other.

Place the cage in the same room where you use to spend most time. Talk to your bird as much as possible and when you change the water and food, try to do it by not stressing the bird too much.

Make sure your bird is used to you and his surroundings. Slowly open the cage, put your hand inside and offer some Millet Spray. The bird may get scared and fly away. It's very important to be patient and keep persisting, until the bird comes to you.

How to make the bird to get used with your hand in its cage:

It is very important to tame one bird at a time. If there are more untamed birds in the cage, they will fly around in the cage and will scare each other.

First, place your hand at the bottom of the cage and leave it there for 10-15 minutes, daily. Repeat this procedure, until the bird got used with your hand in its cage. In this time, it's very important to talk with your bird.

Next, move your hand closer to the bird by touching the perch with your hand. If the bird is flying away, then place your hand back at the bottom of the cage. Do it over and over again, until your feathered friend will except your hand in its cage. Don`t forget that this "step" can take several days or even weeks in order to succeed.

You can start giving your bird millet spray or a bunch of Dandelion leaves or lettuce. If the bird starts eating the millet or the greens, you can go for the next step. Next, you can start hand feeding your bird. Pour some seeds on your palm and slowly move your hand towards the bird. If the bird looks a little bit scared, then pull your hand back and after a few minutes try the trick again. After several trials your bird will eat from your hand.

Step up trick

When your bird is comfortable with your hand close, take a stick and slowly move it towards the bird and press it gently on his abdomen and say "Step up!".
After a few days of practicing and praising, your bird will manage to step up on the stick.
The next step is to move your finger towards the bird and press it gently on his abdomen and say "Step up!". When the bird is able to "step up" on your finger, you will no longer need the stick.
When the bird is tamed enough, take it out of the cage and start practicing in the room.
You can also use clickers with success to achieve the best training results. Budgies usually learn quicker when you're using a clicker. First of all you will need a clicker and some treat/Millet Spray.
When you start training your bird, first give it a treat and in the same time say "well done" or click the clicker. Your parrot will associate these sounds with the treat. You'll have to raise your hand in front of the bird, just like you want the bird to step up on it.
When s/he step up, say "well done" and give to your

bird the treat. Repeat this command for a few times, until the bird will understand it. Once the bird has raised his/her leg on its own to get the treat, wait and give the treat only when the bird is raising its leg a little bit higher.

After a few days you can leave the cage door open and s/he will realise that you are the best friend for him/her. S/he will come out of the cage and will "step up" on your finger. Soon you will observe that your parrot will sit very comfortable on your shoulder, which means that s/he accepted you.

Parrots, in general, love sitting on people's shoulders and love to chew things which decreases their aggression and actual depression problems.

Teach your parrot to play basketball, using a miniature - sized basketball hoop by picking up "an easy to hold ball" and passing it through the tiny basket. Show your bird the basketball and say "Toss!" and then put the basketball through the hoop. Next, hand the ball to your bird and say "Toss!"

If your bird puts the ball through the hoop, say "Well done!" in a happy, excited tone and give the treat to your bird.

How to potty train your bird

Birds may be different in defecating or doing their "business", however it is important to monitor your bird's habits.

In general, birds tend to do their "business" every 5-15 minutes.

Choose a place where you would like your bird to do its "business". Call your bird to step up on your finger and take it over the chosen location. Wait a 1-2 minutes and if the bird has not done her "business", then moves it away and after 5 minutes take the bird back on that specific location, try again and say "Go poop!"

Potty train your budgie may take several weeks to achieve.

Make sure to praise your bird verbally when the bird manage to do its "business" right.

How to train parrots to stop biting

When parrots feel threatened they will react in different ways, like screaming, flapping their wings, running away, growling, hissing, biting, etc…

There are several factors that can make parrots feel threatened like, perturbing them when attention is not wanted, invading their territory, sudden movements, unexpected noises, jealousy. Parrots can also bite when protecting their mate. If your bird has chosen you for a mate, it may feel that unfamiliar persons or new pets, appear as a threat to your safety. In these situations it is best to gradually introduce your bird to the new person or pet, allowing your bird enough time to accept the change.

Parrots who are going through hormonal changes during the breeding season or molting may become annoyed and moody which may lead to biting. You should watch your bird`s body language during these periods and leave your bird alone when attention is not wanted. It is our natural behavior when a bird bites, to put the bird down and then we start to yell at it. In this situation we reinforce the bird to bite us, because that brings the bird more and more attention. When your young parrot try to nibble on your ears, fingers or other body parts you should offer them an acceptable alternative to chew on: apple slice, carrot, block of wood, etc... If the method above doesn't work, then gently blow in their face and in a firm voice tell them "no".

All we want to do is to reinforce and reward good behaviors like doing interactive things, standing on your hand, playing quietly, that are positive and socially acceptable.

For example, choose a toy, a key or an object which could interest your parrot, when s/he is touching that object reward or praise your bird.

After s/he seems to look that s/he understand that command, make it to pick up that object. You have to repeat this game until your parrot will pick it up and will bring you that object.

Training lessons have to be short about 5-10 minutes and to represent a positive experience for you and for your bird.

The rewards (treats) have to be small quantities, but also something that your bird will enjoy to eat, like sunflower seeds or millet. If you offer big rewards to your bird, then s/he will spend too much time to eat them and your training lesson will be interrupted for too long.

If your bird bites you, try hard not to even yell out in pain, just take the bird, put it down and walk away. Your parrot will learn, that when s/he bites you, then s/he will lose your attention.

Make sure your bird have things available to play with, so that s/he will not bite you. Your parrot can't eat and bite, can't shred toys and bite at the same time. Therefore, if you can anticipate the behavior from happening, regardless of what kind of behavior is (biting, screaming) and you can provide some sort of distraction for your bird, it will not bite.

You can place a wooden chopstick within the bird`s rich. When the bird does bite the stick, you should praise it.

After all, your bird will understand that biting a stick is a good thing.

Cages and accessories

When you choose a cage for your bird you have to take into consideration the size and the temperament of your bird, because s/he will spend almost all its time in that cage.

You have to be sure that your bird will be able to fly without any problem between the climbing perches or to flap its wings.

Cage location

Your parrot just adore when you are around him/her, so you'll have to place the cage in the same room where you spend most of your time.

To avoid any possible danger, you'll have to take into consideration a few aspects:
- place the cage near the window, so your parrot can enjoy the natural light;
- avoid placing the cage in air currents;
- avoid placing the cage in the kitchen, especially when you cook, because the steam contains toxic substances that can harm your bird
- don't place the cage near television or near any home audio system

Cages

The cage size is very important for these birds. Square or rectangular cage would be the perfect shape for them.

These parrots are very playful, therefore it is important to offer them a large cage to allow room for toys and exercise.

They also need socialization and play outside the cage. Trimming the wings prevent the escape of the bird.

The cage has to be two or three times bigger than the

bird's wingspan and three times bigger than the bird`s length from head to tail. It has to be big enough for the bird, so it will be able to open its wings and flaps them. Especially for single birds you'll have to equip the cage with toys, mirrors and swings.

You'll have to change the toys very often, to keep your bird from becoming bored. To maintain your parrot's feet health, you must provide proper perches for the bird's feet, otherwise it will be difficult for your parrot to properly hold on to a perch. Your parrot should be able to stand on the perch, without the toes completely touching each other in a circle.

Large metal bird cage on wheels for more than one budgie

If you choose to offer your parrot natural branch perches, make sure that they are without any wild bird droppings and free of insects. You'll have to disinfect them with hot boiled water, before using them. There are also comfortable braided rope perches, which are good choice for your bird to rest on. Grooming perches will keep your bird's beak in shape.

The resistance of the cage is very important, one made of metal is much more resistant than one made of plastic. The space between the bars it's very important, because the bird could get its head, legs or even its beak stuck. When you buy a cage make sure that it's not painted, because parrots will eat the paint, and if the paint is toxic, they can get sick and even die.

This cage is surely enough for two budgies

The minimum suitable size of the cage should be 14 inches Long x 11 inches Wide x 18 inches High (35.56 cm Long x28cm Wide x 45.72 cm High), bar spacing ½" or less.

The cage should be in a corner or against the wall to

give a feeling of security.

The nesting box should be at the highest point in the cage and the entrance hole should be in a shaded position. A ladder must be fixed inside, just below the entrance hole, to allow access up and down from and to the box.

Toys and accessories

The best toys for them are pieces of softwood or perches, ping-pong balls, all kind of unpainted paper-made items, etc... You'll have to provide some items which will help to maintain the physical health condition of your bird:

- acrylic toys with bells attached
- swings and chains which increases the capacity of movement;
- therapeutical perches which helps to maintain the bird's feet healthy;
- perches or any wood made objects which are good for chewing (if you neglect your bird by not offering him/her different objects to chew, could lead to beak deformation)
- a bowl with fresh water for bathe
- various nutritional supplements like cuttlefish bone, seashells, etc...

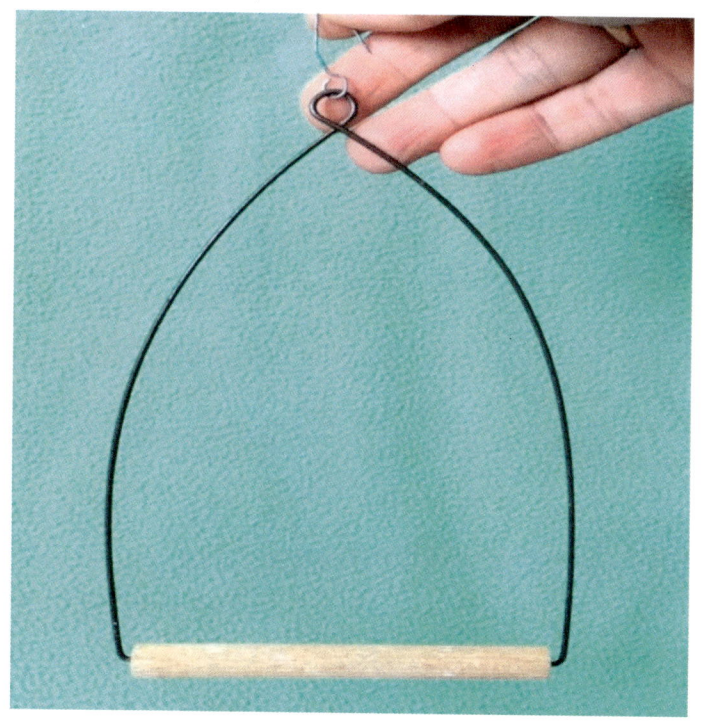

One of the best game that your parrot could play is when s/he has to get out a peanut which was previously hidden inside of a tiny hole of a log.

Your parrot has to chew the log to get inside and to get the peanut. This game makes your bird to concentrate and to work hard to eat.

You can also make your parrot happy by replacing the old toys and perches with new ones. In fact, toys and interactive games which makes your bird to work hard mentally and physically, will keep your bird healthy and svelte.

Cleaning your budgie`s "house"

Your beloved parrot could be easily affected by the bacterias which can live in the cage during the day, that's why you need to clean it every day and a more complex clean is required every week.

The floor of the cage, the food and water recipients should be cleaned daily.

I recommend that the floor of the cage to be covered with kitchen paper towel or paper sheets which can be changed daily. The disinfection of the cage, food and water recipients must be made with hot water weekly.

Don't use disinfection products very often because they are toxic for your parrot! When you do so, be careful and move the bird in a different room.

It's very important to use eye protection glasses and gloves when the disinfection operation is taking place, because it can cause serious injuries.

You can use bleach for disinfection, but be aware to avoid mixing it with other chemical products, because it's very dangerous. You can use the bleach in diluted form : 30 ml of bleach mixed with 250ml of water. This mixture will be very efficient to combat bacterias and viruses. After you finish with the disinfection process, it's very important to rinse well with cold water the recipients and the cage.

You can also disinfect the cage and the feeding utensils with vinegar or baking soda.

Disinfection with vinegar

Vinegar cleans excessive mold, mildew, grease, etc... Vinegar can be used for multiple purposes: to make pickled vegetables, for window cleaning, to disinfect household items and more.

For cage disinfection, mix together 1 liter of water with 1 liter of vinegar or make a solution that is a 1:1 ratio of vinegar to water.

With this solution disinfect the cage, the utensils and don`t forget to rinse well everything with cold water.

How to maintain your budgie`s health

Few advices about how to keep your budgies healthy

The most important condition to keep your birds healthy is a proper diet. Choosing the appropriate cage and the right environment are very important factors. A smaller cage than a usual one may cause agitation and the bird will try to escape.

The cage must be kept clean, to avoid bacterial infestation. Daily flying exercises is also needed.

Watch out, your ornamental plants: philodendron, iris and yellow daffodil could be poisonous for your birds. Cigarette smoke, hair spray (hair lacquer), body spray, furniture spray, vapors of household cleaners like bleach, should be avoided, when the birds are around.

Avoid exposing your cage with your parrot inside when there are dangerous cats around because they can easily knock down the cage.

Learn about the natural habits of your bird. For instance, you can find out if your bird love to have bath more often than showers. Then you'll have to place a bowl filled with water in the cage, or for the other option you'll have to spray him/her with water very often. Try to discover and offer your bird the most favorite and natural foods as possible and make available natural environments for it.

Make regular veterinary examinations, because birds can hide the signs of diseases. In the wild sick birds used to hide any sign of their disease, they even try to eat with the rest of the flocks, because there is a risk to lose their life (the others will steal his food and bite him because they feel his weakness). The cage birds can act the same way, they look like they are healthy, they eat very well, until one day, they could fall off from the perches. Even when they have sharp pains, they don't tend to exteriorize their feelings. The bird plumage can hide the eventually weight losses caused by diseases.

If you recognize the signs presented above, you better visit your avian vet as soon as possible. Sometimes a routine examination can help to discover any latent infection of the bird.

The first sign of disease

There are several physical and behavioral signs about the bird's illness:
- depressed attitude and unusual irritability;
- they sleep more than 10-12 hours per day, with their head hidden under the wing
- they keep their eyes almost shut all the time and the wings hang from the body

- don't have the same stability on their legs and they spend more time as usual on the bottom of the cage
- their appetite is reduced and they are losing weight
- don't clean their plumage and their feet
- excessive cough and sneeze and nose secretion dripping
- the feathers around the beak are dirty
- their feces colour differs from normal and they present diarrhoea
- excessive moulting
- discoloration of the feathers
- breathing difficulties

When you recognize these signs, you should contact your vet doctor for a precise diagnosis.

How to recognize the abnormal droppings

Feces and urine are eliminated by your bird at the same time.

The color of feces depends by the assimilation of the food and it can vary from dark green and brown, to black. On the feces usually there is a white urine patch. If the darker part of the feces is more liquid, then the bird has diarrhoea.

When the urine appears like a lake around the fecal material, there could be kidney problems.

There could be situations when you have to visit your avian vet for routine examinations (check-ups) and because of the stress, the droppings of your bird could have a very liquid form, but just for a short period of time and it will normally pass away. In this case we don't talk about diseases. For a precise examination you better visit your avian vet.

Feather picking and self - mutilation
When a bird moves its beak through the feathers making them clean, then we talk about preening.
But when the bird starts to pay too much attention to its feathers by pulling them out obsessively, then we talk about self-mutilation.

Some of the factors that create this problem are: skin diseases, stress or internal diseases. When the main cause is the skin itchiness, among the special treatments prescribed by your avian vet, you can also apply directly on the bird's skin some anesthetic powder.

In this period you'll have to avoid placing the cage near radiators or in direct sunlight, because the bird's skin will become excessively dry.

Breeding

In the wild budgies breed colonially in tree hollows with narrow entrances, especially in eucalyptus trees and they are usually laying six to eight eggs twice a year. They also make their nests at the roots of trees and even in the ground.

Breeding season starts from June to September in northern Australia and from June to August in southern Australia. Having said that, it is good to know that budgies will start breeding as soon as they find water sources, which is very important in the feeding process of their youngsters.

In captivity, budgies breeding season starts from April to August, but be aware that budgies are capable to breed all year long if there is food and water supply in their cage and if you let them.

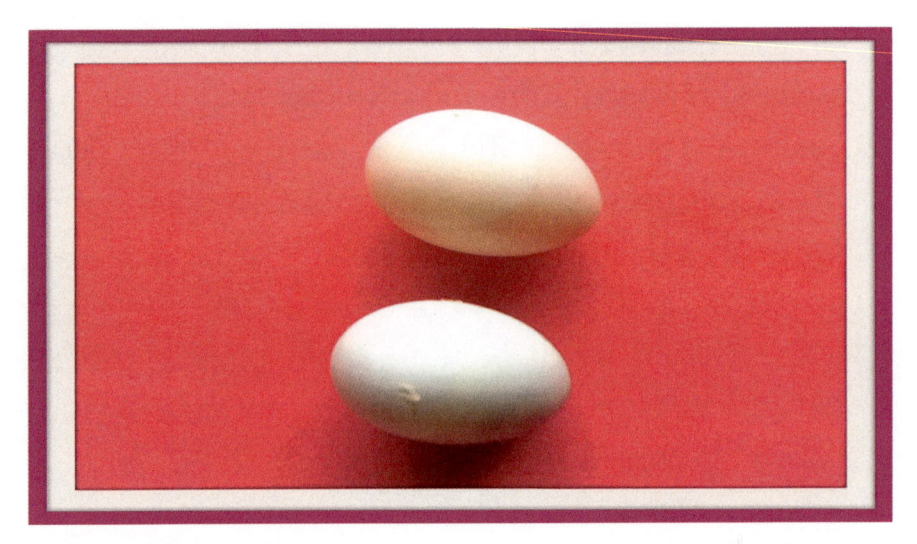

They will breed in shadowy places or in nesting boxes. Budgies usually only raise one brood a season, although if one clutch is lost, the female will usually lay another clutch. In warmer areas they will produce two clutches. In this period the pair will become a little bit aggressive.

Budgies are monogamous birds, which means that they bond with one partner for life. The female usually lays 4-6 eggs (one egg every two days). The egg sitting period usually lasts between 18-21 days. During this period, the male bring her food and feeds her. The hatchlings are blind and naked. The pair will need to be provided with plenty of food, especially soft food to allow them to feed their youngsters.

The youngsters are completely weaned when they are 6 weeks old. By the sixth week the baby budgies become strong enough and completely weaned. At this stage they are ready to leave their nest.

In some color mutations, the youngsters present bar markings on the forehead that disappear with age and their eyes have dark irises, that gradually become gray with age. During breeding season the cere of the male is blue and the female`s is chocolate brown color.

Budgies require deep vertical nesting boxes, with dimensions of 7.5 inches wide x 7.5 inches deep x 10.6 inches high (19cm x 19cm x 27cm). The nesting box should be made of exterior grade plywood. The entrance hole can be round or square with a diameter of 1.96 inches (5 cm).

The nest box should have a removable top lid for nest inspection. Nesting materials such as pine or wood shavings, dried plant materials should cover the bottom of the nest box.

How to setup the breeding cage

The size of the breeding cage should be at least 24 inches Lx16inchesWx16inchesH(60cmL x 40cmW x 40cmH) with two perches made of solid wood. You will have to setup the cage with a mineral block, a cuttlefish bone, food and water dishes, a nest box and a well balanced seed and pellet diet.

Once you have selected the pair that you want to breed, I recommend to pay very close attention to their behavior for the next few days. You have to make sure that the pair is compatible, otherwise, if they don't like each other, they might fight and kill each other.

Any underaged budgie (any under 12 months) should never be force-breed.

If the female accepted the male then she will allow the male to follow her around.

If the male likes the female then he will bob his head with enthusiasm. If the pair preen and feed each other then it means that they are compatible.

Mating rituals

Before they mate, the male will have a specific behavior. He will chirp endlessly, jump from perch to perch and will bob his head. The male will move near the female, tapping his beak against the females beak.

The excited female will stay still and will raise her tail, whilst the male will move his vent against hers to inseminate her. The mating process is short and it is repeated a few times during a day.

Molting

The molting process can take place once or twice per year, which usually does not have any effect on the bird's flying capacity.

The natural molting happens when the warm season ends and the colder season starts to appear. In this period of the year birds will change all their feathers. The molting will take place gradually, and it could happen only after they have hatched their eggs and after rearing their youngsters (April - August).

Camomile flowers (Matricaria Chamomilla)

The molting process is influenced by the hormones of thyroid gland and the genital organs. In this period they'll need proper diet like camomile tea (Matricaria Chamomilla), St John's wort tea (Hypericum Perforatum), amino acid like methionine, hemp seeds and vitamins like A, D, E. They also become very stressed when molting takes place, and makes them vulnerable to new diseases. In this period they`re cleaning themselves persistently and have a more quiet behavior. When normal molting is taking place, there should never be bald patches present on the bird's body. The new feathers that are replacing the old feathers, are called blood feathers. If the blood feathers are cut or injured they can bleed in excess.

If your bird has broken blood feathers, you'll have to ask your avian vet for help. All he has to do is to pull the broken feather out and apply some pressure with a gauze pad to stop the bleeding. When your parrot is molting it could have many pin feathers present especially on the back of its head because a single parrot can`t preen the normally present feather sheaths from the back of the head. You can help your parrot by removing gently the feather sheaths with your index finger and thumb. You have to be very careful when you are doing this operation, because it could be very painful for your bird.

How to take care of the beak and the nails of your budgie

The bird's beak and nails grow continuously, so you have to take care of them, throughout your bird's life.

To prevent the beak to grow excessively you need to cut it back carefully with a strong pair of scissors.

Grooming perches are a very good choice and they are available in different shapes and sizes which will keep the bird`s beak in good shape. Be careful because these perches are not comfortable for the bird's feet. If the bird is sitting for a long period of time on these perches, the bottom of their feet may become swollen and excessively dry. Unfortunately this problem may lead to infection of their feet. So be aware, and make sure that your bird always have two comfortable wooden perches installed in its cage to rest on.

The cuttlefish bone is known to be a very good source of calcium, which must be present in the bird's every day diet and it is also good for the maintenance of the beak.

When trimming process is taking place, for a safer procedure (to avoid injuries of the bird), you should always have someone helping you out.

Parrots have a predisposition for excessive beak growth, therefore you'll have to cut it very often if there is no grooming perches installed in their cages.

Sadly some parrots which don't get the necessary care and don't have grooming perches in their cages, could die because of their untreated and overgrown beak.

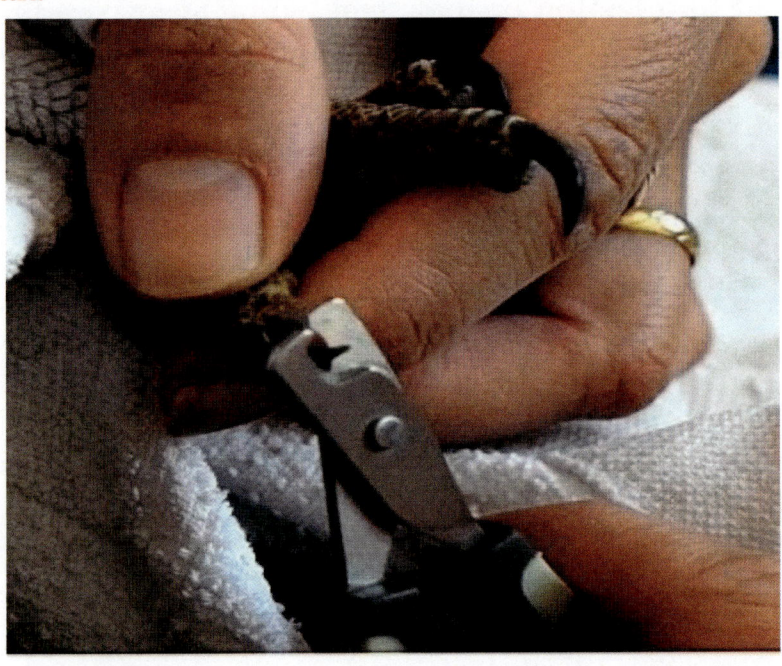

Before trimming the beak, dab it with slightly warm glycerin or olive oil.

When nails overgrow, you need to cut them very carefully with a special scissor without causing any injuries. Overgrown nails lead to instability on the perches or even the impossibility to move around.

When trimming the nails it is best to cut off a little bit at a time. You have to know that the birds nails contain (at their base) very fine blood vessels and nerves, which makes them very sensitive.

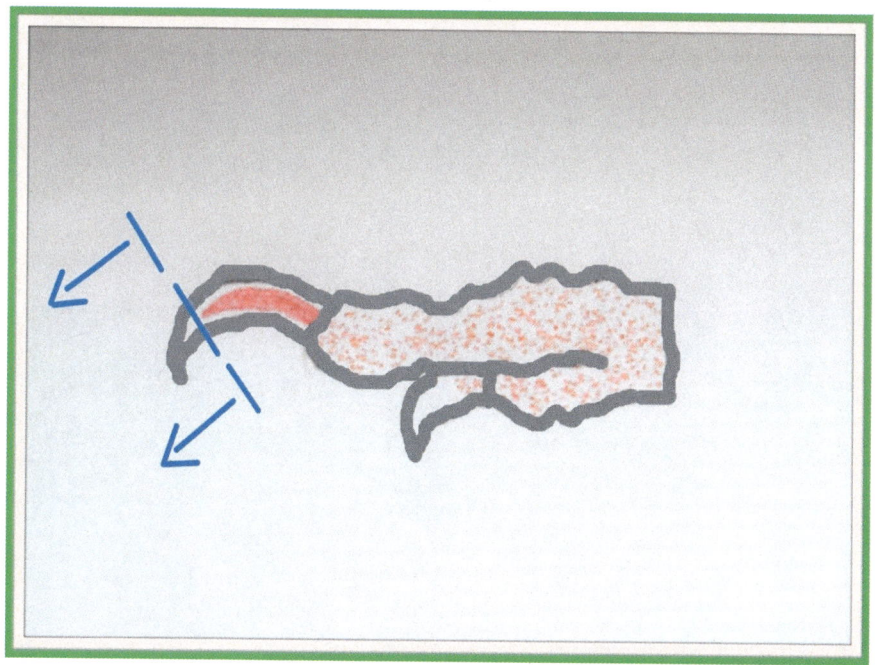

If by mistake, you cut too much from the bird's nails, they will bleed and the bird will feel the same pain as we do when we over cut our nails. In this case you can stop the bleeding by using cotton buds soaked in vitamin K or C.

For a better result, when you cut the nails, you can grease your bird's fingers and nails with comestible oil, to soften them.

How to clip your budgie's wings

If your parrot mostly lives in an aviary and you don't interact with it, then clipping the wing is unnecessary. The main purpose of wing clipping is to prevent rapid and upward flight. Wing clipping is safe if it is performed properly.

If you don't know how to clip your bird's wing, the best way is to find an avian vet, who is experienced in the art of wing clipping.

If you decide to do it by yourself then you'll have to study about the bird's wing shape and about terminology of its feathers. You will also need a competent assistant who will help you holding the bird. Avoid clipping the primary and secondary coverts, and secondary feathers on both wings.

With the help of your assistant wrap the bird in a towel and hold it by the back of its neck. Be careful, the bird's chest must not be restricted because it will not be able to breathe. Further on, carefully liberate one wing, which has to be held at the base of the humerus and not by the feathers. If you do not hold the wing correctly, you can cause serious injuries, when the bird tries to flap its wing.

You can leave intact the last three primary feathers (P10,P9,P8) and clip the next four primary feathers (P7,P6,P5,P4) or you can clip the first four primary feathers (P7,P8,P9,P10) and you can leave the other primary feathers intact. Same process can be repeated on the other wing.

Bathing your parrot

In the wild, parrots can take a bathe in rainy days by opening their wings and tail sideways or they can have a bathe in little natural ponds formed on uneven ground. In captivity, you have to provide different ways to keep your bird clean. You can spray them or you can give them a shower, but you should be careful because the upper respiratory tract and the sinuses are quite exposed. You can provide them artificial ponds by using not too deep water bowls or you can also use the sink or the bathtub.

However, your bird will still love to have a bathe in its drinking water bowl. Sometimes your parrot will get dirty and greasy, in these kind of situations you'll have to use special shampoos.

The best shampoos are those for the children. There are also several special products for your bird, but be careful of those which contains oils and perfumes, because your bird could perceive them as detrimental substances and it may start to pull out his/her own feathers. You'll have to dilute a little bit of shampoo in the bathing water and easily sprinkle your bird with it until it became all wet. Leave the bird about five minutes in a warm place, then rinse it well with clean warm water. If your bird is excessively dirty (oil, ink, liquid glue, etc..) then you'll have to visit your avian vet as soon as possible.

The special needs of the parrots

Flying exercises

Parrots belong to flying birds category, so they'll need to fly very often, therefore, if you have a small cage in your house, you'll have to assure them with almost daily flying exercises, to maintain their well being. A room with well closed windows will surely be enough for them.

You have to avoid to agglomerate a small cage with lots of birds and toys. If you can't afford a bigger cage, then one pair of parrots should be enough for you. As long as they are two, they will do just fine.

Free flight will prevent muscle atrophy of the wings and chest, and it will maintain the bird in a good physical condition. You should allow your bird a minimum of 2-3 hours daily free flight, so that the bird can play, fly and stretch its muscles. When you leave the bird outside of the cage, serious precautions have to be taken, because your bird could be everywhere, for example on the couch where it can be crashed, when it is hiding between the pillows.

The kitchen represents another problem for them. You should not leave the birds in the kitchen, especially when you are cooking, because they can get burnt by falling into a hot pan.

They love to sit on top of the doors, so you have to be careful when you close the door behind you.

Before the first flight, you have to place your bird close to the window to get used with it, otherwise it will try to fly through the window and serious accidents could happen. You can also cover the window with curtains to avoid accidents.

In the wild, parrots use to "work" to provide their food, to build their nest, to fly and care for their young ones. Therefore, you will have to make sure that your parrot will perform some exercises for five minutes, a few times every day.

Wing flapping: try to lower your hand up and down to encourage flapping. You can swing your parrot around in a circle or back and forth by making your bird to flap its wings a few times a day. You can also place a blanket on the floor and chase your parrot around. They will love this game.

You can also encourage your bird to dance with you and with your children. Your parrot will be very happy to dance and jump around, which will make him/her consume its energy. Make sure that children and parrots are supervised.

Bedding materials

In the wild the birds have less contact with their droppings, because they have unlimited space.

In captivity, their droppings could affect the birds health by distribution of microbes and parasites.

The loose sand or absorbent paper are the best bedding materials. You should avoid using newspaper, because it contains lead (chemical substance), which could be dangerous for your bird.

To help with digestion, parrots will need daily portion of grit in their cages. The grit will have to be changed daily, because it might get contaminated with their own droppings.

The everyday life of a budgie

During the day, budgies will play by climbing on perches, sing or will wait for the owners to return home.

In the wild parrots get up at sunrise and go to sleep at sunset. In captivity you have to respect the day and night program of the bird. So you have to be sure that your bird will spend most of the day in a room exposed to light. Therefore, you can place the cage close to the window.

At night time, they will need a room without any illumination and noise source, in order for them to have a good sleep.

In case that you stay up for long and you have to use the light in the same room where the birds are, you better cover the cage with a thin piece of curtain material to help them sleep. When the weather is hot, you can cover the half part of the cage, with the same piece of curtain material, which will help the bird to take shelter from direct sunlight.

Inappropriate perches

In the wild the birds sit on different sizes of branches, which are very comfortable for them.

In captivity they spend almost all the time on the perch, which could be too slippery, too thick or too thin for the birds feet. All these imperfections can cause swelling of the feet and deformities of the joints. To avoid these problems, you can place different sized branches in the cage, but first you'll have to peel their bark. These branches must be disinfected by pouring hot water on them.

It is good to have different sized perches in the cage because they will stimulate the blood circulation and they will exercise the parrots feet.

First aid kit for your budgie

It is very important to have a first aid kit in your house, because unexpected accidents could happen sometimes. The first thing that you will have to do, is to call your avian vet. In case that your bird require immediate medical care, you have to be ready to use your first aid kit. In cases like burn or injury of the bird you will have to take immediate action, before the vet inspection is taking place.

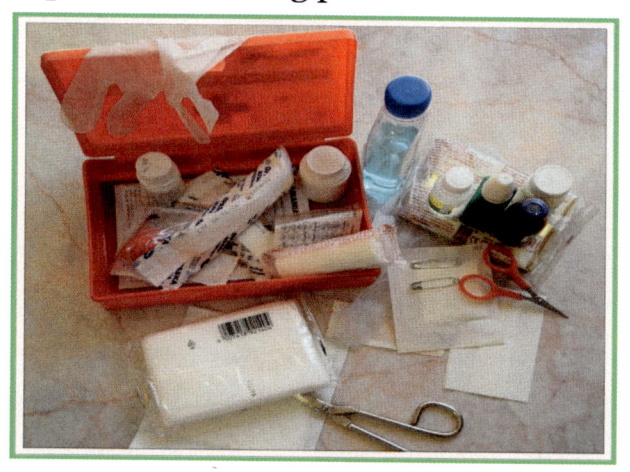

The first aid kit must contain the following items:
- electric bird pillow, to warm up the bird to treat shocks; in case that your bird is very sick don't leave it unattended on the pillow, because the danger of overheating might happen.
- Pedialyte (electrolyte solution for children), this kind of solution has to be given at room temperature
- eye drops (medication) and eye wash (to clean the eyes)
- eyedropper
- cotton swabs and balls to clean the open wound
- scissors
- gauze rolls to bandage scratches, burns or open wounds
- tweezers to remove broken blood feathers

- antiseptic wipes
- betadine or iodine solution
- medical tape
- masking tape
- 3% hydrogen peroxide solution to clean wounds. When you clean the wound for the first time, you'll have to use the undiluted form of the solution. Further on, you will have to dilute the hydrogen peroxide solution with water 1:10.
- medical first aid pen flashlight, to see inside of the bird's mouth
- antibiotic ointment to prevent infection of cuts and scratches
- syringe, feeding tubes, pipettes. You have to be well prepared before you use feeding tubes.
- towels
- hand feeding formula (mature birds can get 5% of their body weight at one feeding, once or twice per day).
- latex gloves
- animal poison control center phone number
- magnifying glass
- heating lamp
- bird`s medical records
- parrot's first aid book

How to hand feed a baby budgie

The optimum period to start hand feeding baby budgies is by the age of 3 weeks old. After they hatch, the chicks must spend the first 3 weeks of their lives with their mother to be fed with her crop milk. The crop milk is very essential in development of the baby budgies, because it contains a lot of nutrients and antibodies.

If you decide to hand feed your baby budgie, you can do it at 3 weeks of age. The maximum quantity of food which has to be given to a baby budgie before the weaning period, has to be 10% of its body weight.

The crop of most baby parrots usually gets empty between 3-4 hours. You will have to stop feeding the bird during night time, between midnight and 6 o'clock, (pause of 6 hours), period which will allow the crop to empty of residual food. In this time you'll have enough time to get rest. As the baby parrot grows, you will have to reduce the number of feeding times, but you will have to increase a little bit more the quantity of food. The most important thing is to control the quantity of food offered at each meal. Do not offer more food than 10% of the bird's body weight in a meal.

As the baby parrot grows, it will gradually refuse to be hand feed. It is also good to know that hand fed budgies might be weaned only at 10 weeks old. When you are at the stage of only 2-3 hand feedings per day, offer your bird solid food (softened pellets) or cooked food. In 2-3 weeks time, your bird should be able to get used with solid food and you can completely skip the evening meals.

How to prepare the hand feeding formula:

Use commercially prepared hand feeding formula which is specifically created for budgie babies.

You should use a thermometer to ensure that the hand feeding formula is warm enough (about 102 to 105 degrees Fahrenheit).

Use the microwave to heat up the water, add a measured amount of formula and stir. Make sure you feed at the right temperature. Baby parrots develop much better on a thin formula rather than a thick one. There are two most common methods of feeding: by syringe or spoon. Allow the bird to breath between bites of food and stop feeding when the crop is nicely rounded.

During weaning period offer your baby budgie veggies, seeds, fruits and good quality pellets. Sprouted grains and seeds are also a good start in weaning your baby parrot, because the softened shell of the seeds and grains is easier to break. Place a separate water dish next to his food. Any remains must be removed after 3 hours. At 9-10 weeks of age your baby parrot should be placed on a single hand feeding per day. At this time pellets and seed mix should be its favorite food. Serve fruits and veggies cut in small pieces.

You can serve warm moistened pellets early in the morning at 8am and 4pm on the afternoon.

At the age of 12 weeks old your bird should be eating on its own.

During weaning period some babies can lose up to 15% of their weight.

It is important to keep an eye on your young bird regularly, regarding feeding. Watch your young bird weight, until it is 5 months old. Take your bird in your hand at least once a day and feel its breast bone by moving your hand from side to side across his/her chest. A healthy young parrot should have its breast bone covered with soft muscles on each side of it.

When you want to bring home a young budgie, make sure the feed pots are placed on the bottom of the cage. The climbing skill are not yet developed and so the easiest way to feed themselves will be from the pots placed on the bottom of the cage. Set up the cage with the perches placed down low, until your bird learns to climb around.

Other foods can also be offered to your baby, like chopped hard boiled egg, boiled rice or pasta, biscuit crumbs, millet spray, boiled sweet potato mash.

Here is a delicious recipe for young Budgies:
1 and 1/2 cups fresh corn
1 cup brown rice
1/2 cup dried mango or banana
2 and 1/2 tbsp raisins
3 and 1/2 tbsp split lentils or peas
2 and 1/2 tbsp unsalted, chopped pumpkin seeds
1 tsp dried powdered milk
Bring 0.5 liters of water to boil, add all contents, cover and boil gently for 30 minutes. Serve warm or cool.

Vitamin and mineral excess or deficiency

Insufficient or too much quantity of vitamin intake can cause serious health problems to the birds. Bird owners must provide them with an optimal intake of vitamins and minerals.

Vitamin A

Vitamin A deficiency is considered to be the main cause of diseases at cage birds. In the bird's body, the carotene is transformed in vitamin A.
Sources of provitamin A: fish fat or cod liver oil; carrots, green plants, vegetables, sunflower seeds;
Diseases: avitaminosis A (A vitamin deficiency):
- drying of the surface of the eyeball;

- eyelid edema;
- infections of the mucous membranes;
- rhinitis;
- sinusitis;
- white membranes inside the beak;
- kidney problems and gout (gout occurs in birds when uric acid level becomes too high in their bloodstream);
- swollen feet;
- diarrhoea;
- fluffed plumage;
- in molting period the slow growth of feathers ;

Properties: protects the mucous membranes, the eyes and skin;

Administration: fish fat or cod liver oil 3-4 drops through the beak;

Vitamin B complex:

Sources of vitamin B: cereal germs, rice bran, carrots, oranges, other fruits, beer yeast;

The beer yeast must be dissolved in warm water before the administration. The preventive doses must be administered daily, until the bird will be perfectly healthy: 5-10 years old bird must have 50 mg beer yeast/day; 11-20 years old bird must have 100-150 mg beer yeast /day; 21-30 years old bird must have 200-250 mg beer yeast/day; 31-40 years old bird must have 300-350 mg beer yeast/day; 41-50 years old bird must have 400-450 mg beer yeast/day; 51-60 years old bird must have 500-550 mg beer yeast/day; 60-70 years old bird must have 550-600 mg beer yeast/day; 70 years old bird must have 650-800 mg beer yeast/day.

Diseases: the bird can't keep its head straight;
- avitaminosis B1 (B1 vitamin deficiency): slowing growth rate, body weight loss, nerve problems, paralysis, spasms, digestive disorders, diarrhoea;
- Properties of vitamin B complex: it should be offered during hatching period, in growth period, in prolonged treatments with antibiotics, to protect the intestinal flora;
- B5- is recommended in circulatory disorders;
- B12- is recommended in development period of the youngsters and in agitation and depression of adult birds;

Administration of B5 and B12 is given in liquid form, a couple of drops through the beak or in drinking water. You must add 1-2 ml of B complex in 50-100 ml of water for 3-5 days.

Vitamin C

Sources of vitamin C: green plants, bananas, grapes, blackcurrant, rose hips, parsley;

Diseases: the small blood vessels become very fragile, hematomas, tiredness;
Properties of vitamin C: increases immunity, strengthens the capillary wall;
Administration: feeding the bird with green plants

Vitamin D

Sources of vitamin D: green plants, fish flour, beer yeast; exposure of the bird to natural sunlight;
Diseases: slow development, fluffed plumage, rachitis, bone fragility, calcium deposits, lack or softening of the egg shell;
Administration: fish fat or cod liver oil - first a few drops through the beak, then mixed with food ;

Vitamin K

Sources of vitamin K: hemp seeds, dill, fruits, spinach,
Diseases: slow clotting - prolonged bleeding in subcutaneous tissue (if the bird is injured or during a surgery)
Properties: it is important in blood clotting;

Vitamin E

Sources of vitamin E: maize, cereal germs, vegetables;
Diseases: decrease of fecundity - atrophy of embryo in egg; loss of coordination of muscles, walking in circles.

Intoxication of the cage birds

Intoxication with:

disinfection substances: the bird has difficulty in breathing, it has discoloured eyes. The bird's life is in danger!

soap or deodorants: they contain a substance which could lead to temporary blindness. Wash the affected area with cold water.

alcohol: the bird is vomiting, it has fluffy feathers, stays in the corner of the cage, it's losing balance. The sick and old birds could die because of their weakened immune system; the healthy birds could recover by themselves.

toxic plants: digestive symptoms: diarrhoea. You need to introduce green plants in your bird's diet.

nicotine (cigarette buts): it can affect the nervous system, causing death. Don't leave cigarettes near the birds.

salt (and salty food): the bird is very thirsty, it is agitated and shaking. You'll need to administrate lots of water through the bird's beak. The bird might also need laxatives. In severe situations, the bird could die.

teflon (from frying pans): suffocation and death in 30 minutes. Avoid keeping the bird in the kitchen. In case of accidents move the bird outside and call your vet as soon as possible.

lead (newspapers, lead-based paint): green coloured diarrhoea (even the presence of blood), the kidneys, the bone's marrow and the nervous system are affected. If the accident is discovered in time, the administration of an antidote is required - calcium EDTA (aminopolycarboxylic acid). Caution must be taken when using this antidote because of its side-effects.

When the bird swallow toxic substances its life is in danger. The most common solutions to overcome these problems are:

The owner must administer some milk with a dropper and after that, the bird will start vomiting in short time.

Another solution is the administration of medicinal coal. You'll have to dissolve 5 grams of medicinal coal in 50 ml of water. This preparation will need to be administered through the beak. Once you have made the operations described above, after one hour, you'll have to administer some oily purgatives, oil or castor oil.

The most common diseases in budgerigars

Sadly, these cute, small parrots may become sick if we don't care for them properly or we don't recognize the disease in its early stages. It is very important to recognize the bird's illness symptoms in time and this way we can keep our birds healthy and happy.

Budgies are exposed to several diseases, some of them are treatable, while others can't be treated. Usually is difficult to observe if anything goes wrong by simply looking at the bird. Birds don't externalize their feelings when they are sick, because they behave instinctively.

In the wild, sicks birds can become preys very easy if they are not vigilant enough. For this reason, they act like they are perfectly healthy.

This unfortunate event could happen with our pet birds. When their immune system collapses, their body become so weakened, that they could fall off from the perch and could die. To avoid such drama, the best thing to do is to prevent, recognize and cure the disease.

To avoid massive infestation, when we buy new birds, it is advisable to quarantine them. The isolated birds must be watched closely and the dropping sample should be wrapped in glad wrap, then foil.

You should send the dropping sample to specialized laboratories for psittacosis and other tests.

If the test results shows that the bird is contaminated with bacteria or parasites then you should treat the new bird.

Doing this way you avoid contamination of other birds.

The quarantine period should last at least 30 days. It is advisable to do a fecal test twice.

The first test should be done right after you have purchased the bird. The second test must be done, after 30 days of quarantine. By doing this, there will be no risk of contamination of the other healthy birds. Be aware, that the fecal and crop test results are not 100% precise and this is why you need to repeat the test twice: in the first and last week of quarantine.

Foot abscess in budgies

The main cause of this disease is the circulatory disorder of blood vessels in the feet, caused by insufficient movement, inappropriate perches and avitaminosis A (lack of green food and fruits).

First, the abscess forms on the heel (the backward-pointing joint) or under a toe (a pressure zone). The skin become very thin, the wound appears and soon it will be covered with crust. The affected foot is swollen and it's very warm. The wound become an open injury filled with pus. The crust has to be removed surgically and the affected foot will be treated with medicated ointment. The affected bird will be supervised for 10 days. The bandage has to be changed at every 2-3 days. Injection with multivitamins stimulates the healing process. To spare the other foot, the perches must be wrapped with paper towel or with bandages to make them softer and they have to be fixed at the end of perches with adhesive tape. All the perches from the cage must be wrapped, otherwise the bird will hesitate to sit on them.

If there are not pustules filled with pus on the bird's foot, it's enough to use ointment with vitamin A or with fish fat (grease) daily. During this treatment the presence of the grit is not necessary in the cage, because it will stick on the bird's affected foot and it will stop the healing process.

Free flight is necessary daily for 1-2 hours. This way the circulatory system and the blood circulation in the feet will be stimulated. The lack of movement and the overweight body of the bird will have negative effects on the feet.

Gout

When uric acid level becomes too high in the bird's blood stream, gout occurs. Birds usually don't produce too much urine. The uric acid is removed from the blood by the kidneys and eliminated through the urine. When the kidneys don't work properly, the level of uric acid becomes too high in the blood stream and it will become crystallized.

In articular gout, the uric acid crystallizes in the joints, ligaments and tendon sheaths, forming white nodules which could be very painful. The feet are swollen and their color will become red-violet. When the uric acid crystallizes in the tissues, it will form small, white nodules.

In visceral gout, uric acid deposits are found in the liver, kidneys, spleen and air sacs.

High level of calcium and protein that is present in the bird`s organism is the cause of gout.

Chemicals that are present in the tap water is another possible cause for gout. Tap water should be filtered before it is offered to the bird.

High dose of vitamin A and lots of fluids may be given to the affected bird. Because of the swollen feet and painful nodules the bird may be unable to perch and so it will remain on the floor of the cage. The food and water bowls should be placed to be easily accessible. This way, we help the bird to eat and drink without any problem. The cage has to contain little wrapped platforms to help the bird to sit comfortable.

Nodules could be eliminated surgically when they have a specific size. In this case it's not recommended anesthesia, because it could harm the affected kidneys.

Enteritis (Inflammation of the intestines)

Enteritis represent the inflammation of the intestines and it's one of the most frequent cause of mortality in cage and aviary birds.

The main causes of enteritis are:
- Nutrition (bad quality food; inadequate composition of the food)
- Intoxications
- Toxic plants, lead, etc...
- Intestinal parasites
- Tapeworms, eelworms, coccidia can harm the intestinal mucus;
- Viruses (There are different kind of viruses: Paramyxoviruses and hepatitis viruses, which can also cause enteritis)
- Bacterial infections (Salmonellosis and E. coli are pathogenic bacterias which are the main causes of the enteritis)

The main symptom of the enteritis is diarrhoea. The feathers around the cloaca are dirty, the bird is lethargic, sad and sleeps too much. The affected bird will drink much water, because it is dehydrated. Laboratory investigations (bacteriological and parasitological analyses) will have to be done to discover the main cause of the enteritis.

Meanwhile, the bird has to be placed in a warm place, it will need infusions and forced feeding. Injection with vitamins will strengthen the immune system of the bird. The avian vet will prescribe the proper antibiotics treatments for your bird.

Obesity

Obesity could lead to serious health problems like heart and circulatory system disorders, joint problems, modification of the internal organs like fatty liver and constipation. The main causes are the lack of free flight, loneliness and overfeeding with flax and rape seeds.

A few things we can do to avoid obesity are: the introduction of lettuce and other healthy greens in the bird's diet and to increase the frequency of free flight in the room.

You can replace the drinking water with dandelion tea, for 20 days. The obese bird will have to receive only half part of the usual daily seeds portion. Green food and fruits can be offered daily.

Iodine deficiency or goiter

Iodine deficiency appears in those budgies that are fed only with seeds. When the bird is suffering from iodine deficiency, the thyroid glands may be affected by increasing in their size.

In other term the malformed thyroid gland is called goiter. The enlarged gland may press the trachea and esophagus.

Symptoms of goiter are: difficulty in breathing and swallowing, voice changes, weight loss, vomiting, poor feather quality, lethargy, visible swelling in the neck, convulsions, sudden death.

Treatment consist of iodine solution that is added in the bird`s drinking water. In severe cases iodine solution may be injected in the bird's body.

To prevent iodine deficiency, make sure that your bird receives the adequate quantity of iodine in its diet. Iodine based mineral blocks or iodine pecking stones are also available in pet stores and should be placed in the bird's cage. The best natural remedies which contain iodine, are seaweeds or kelp. There are several types of seaweeds.

Excessive use of seaweed may provide the body with too much iodine and may interfere with thyroid function!

You can find them especially in dried form in specialized stores or you can order them online.

You can learn how to use natural remedies (including seaweed), in your bird's diet, from one of my books:

Natural remedies for Ringneck Parakeets: Herbal Teas.

Even though the title does not refer to budgies, (although we know that budgies are parakeets as well) you can definitely use all the information found in this book to maintain your budgie`s well being.

The most efficient and healthiest method of using seaweed is the powder form.

Psittacosis or parrot fever

Psittacosis is caused by a bacteria called Chlamydia psittaci and it can be identified at more than 130 species of birds: parrots, canaries, pigeons, geese, ducks, turkeys, chickens, pheasants, doves, seagulls, etc... This nasty disease can wipe out many birds in a few days from breeders aviaries if the disease is not recognized in time.

Symptoms of psittacosis are: lack of appetite, weight loss, tiredness, conjunctivitis, fever, respiratory disorders, white-green or bloody colored diarrhoea. It is transmitted directly from bird to bird or by infested sand, fluff and droppings. The sick bird may shiver, it's lethargic and present discharge from the nose and eyes.

Before the administration of the antibiotics, laboratory analysis of the droppings and blood sample will be necessary for a precise diagnosis.

To combat this disease, separate the sick birds from healthy ones and disinfect the cage. You must use protective equipment to avoid infestation. After the disinfection process, the protective equipments must be sterilized.

The affected birds have to be treated with Tetracycline or Doxycycline for 3 weeks. At humans the symptoms are as like flu with a strong pneumonia.

Aspergillosis

Aspergillosis is a respiratory disease, caused by infection with a fungus, called Aspergillus. Damp bedding and food, inadequate cage cleaning and humidity can increase the number of fungal spores which are inhaled from the environment. Aspergillosis develops in lungs and air sacs of the bird. Open mouthed breathing and respiratory problems (wheezing and whistling) are signs of an increased severity of the disease.

Treatment: Stamycin in drinking water; potassium iodide in drinking water.

External parasites

External parasites or ectoparasites can be divided into lice, mites and the rest.

Lice infestations appears as small, brownish colored insects that can be seen moving through your bird's feathers. Sometimes you can't see lice with your naked eyes, you just simply notice excessive itching in your bird. Bird lice lay their eggs at the base of the feather and the egg developing period could take for up to 6 weeks.

Common symptoms of feather lice in budgies are: feather ruffling, restless behavior, scratching, consistent preening and feather damage.

The cage, utensils and the toys must be disinfected. You must also clean the surrounding cage area to avoid reinfestation.

Feather lice can be treated with Pyrethrin. It can be used by spraying the plumage, especially under the wings, the vent area and on the back. After 2 minutes, hold the bird over a white sheet, ruffle the feathers and observe the lice drop off the bird.

After 5-7 days repeat this procedure to be sure that there are no more parasites on the bird's plumage.

Daily bathing will help prevent infestations of lice.

Scaly Face / Leg mite

The most common mite seen on birds is Cnemidocoptes- the Scaly Face / Leg mite, which feeds on keratin, the protein that makes up the surface layer of the skin, beak and feet. Left untreated the Scaly Face/Leg mite can cause disruption of the growth areas of the beak, leading to distortion of the beak. Thickening of the scales on the legs can lead to pain.

Massive infestation leads to total or partial loss of feathering.

The combat of parasites can be done with treatments using Ivermectin or Moxidectin, which can be applied on the skin on the back of the neck or in the bird's drinking water.

These type of parasites don't have any effects on humans.

Syringophilus bipectinatus

which feed on feather and skin excess and they can be located between live feathers brushes and tail feathers. Malformation of feathers, may occur, which can be treated with Ivermectin.

Dermanyssus gallinae, the red bird mite appears mostly at aviary birds, which do not live on the bird's body. During the day, they are hiding in cracks and crevices around aviaries. Massive infestation takes place during summer.

The treatment must be done with insecticides in aviary, before the birds were previously moved. After disinfection you need to rinse the aviary with water. The birds will be treated with Pyrethrum powder. Decontamination will be repeated after 7 days.

To prevent parasitic reinfestation after you finished the prescribed treatment with your bird, you'll have to thoroughly clean the bird's cage by disinfecting all its surfaces, corners and bars of the cage.

Internal parasites

Trichomoniasis or Canker (Trichomonas gallinae)

This parasite is located in the sinuses, mouth, throat, crop, intestine and liver of the bird. Among domestic birds, there are also wild birds which are infested with this kind of internal parasite (sparrows, vultures, seagulls, wild doves, etc...).

In pigeons, this disease is commonly called canker.

Symptoms of Trichomoniasis: white or yellow cheesy-looking nodules inside of the mouth and throat; reduced appetite; excessive mucus in the mouth, esophagus and crop; vomiting; dehydration; weight loss; diarrhoea; respiratory disorders; even death.

Treatments: you must gently remove the cheesy deposits from the bird's mouth and apply some tincture of glycerin-iodine solution (1%trypaflavine).

Trichomoniasis is very contagious disease and can be spread through the beak (when they feed each other), through the food and drinking water. If the disease is recognized in time (is located only in the crop and the mouth), then immediate treatment with Dimetridazole is required.

Dimetridazole for 3-5 days or Metronidazole (Flagyl) twice daily for 5-6 days or Ronidazole for 7 days.

You must separate the infected birds from the others. The cage and the accessories must be disinfected with hot water.

Toxoplasmosis

Toxoplasmosis is an infection caused by a protozoan parasite called Toxoplasma gondii. This parasite can infect humans and any warm - blooded animals, including birds. Domestic cats are exposed to this infection, if they consume uncooked meat containing Toxoplasmosis gondii tissue cysts.

Consuming food or drink that contains sporozoites oocysts (one of the infectious stage of Toxoplasmosis gondii) will cause infection of the whole gastrointestinal tract.

Symptoms of Toxoplasmosis are fever, respiratory dysfunction, diarrhoea, paresis, paralysis, convulsion.

Treatments of Toxoplasmosis: administration of sulfonamides; antibiotics (Clindamycin). Disinfection of the cage or aviary is required.

Cats should be fed only with dry or cooked food. Contamination could be prevented by disinfection of cats. Cat litter box should be emptied daily.

When gardening, it is recommended to wear gloves, therefore the vegetables should be washed thoroughly before eating or offered to your bird, because they may have been contaminated with cat feces.

Tapeworms

Tapeworms which lives in the infested bird's body, eliminate their eggs through the bird's feces.

The eggs are consumed by intermediate hosts (earthworms, snails and insects like grasshoppers, ants, beetles, flies, etc...). Inside of the intermediate hosts a small embryo develops in the eggs but does not hatch immediately.

When the bird is eating the infected insects or worms, the larvae in the egg reaches infective stage within 2 to 3 weeks and they will become tapeworms in the bird's body. The eggs are consumed by intermediate hosts (earthworms, snails and insects like grasshoppers, ants, beetles, flies, etc...).

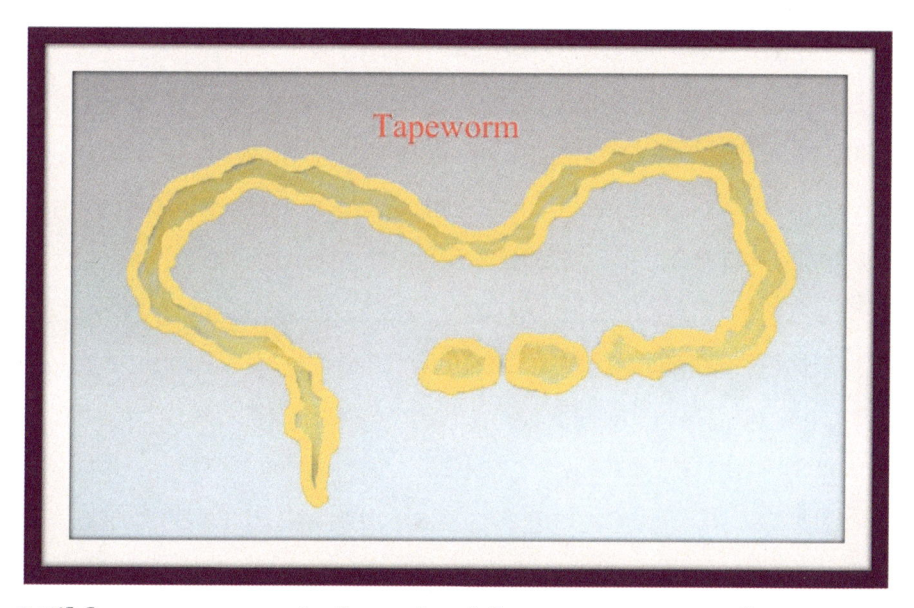

Tapeworm

Wild parrots are infested with tapeworms when they eat insects and worms directly from the wild. Wild parrots which were recently imported (captured from the wild) may have a prophylactic treatment with Praziquantel. Infestation with tapeworms is uncommon in domestically raised parrots.

Threadworms or Capillaria

There are several species of Capillaria. One of them are the threadworms. Threadworms can be found in the lower intestinal tract causing severe inflammation of it. Disinfection of the cage and of the utensils is required with hot water and treatments with Mebendazole may be used.

Coccidiosis (Eimeria)

Coccidiosis is a disease which is produced by parasites which are developing in the bird's intestinal tract. There are 9 species of Coccidia which belong to the genus Eimeria and can infect different parts of the intestine: Eimeria tenella, Eimeria acervulina, Eimeria mivati, Eimeria mitis, Eimeria necatrix, Eimeria maxima, Eimeria brunetti, Eimeria praecox, Eimeria hagani. It can affect youngsters between 10 days and three months old.

Treatment of coccidiosis: administration of polivitamines, sulfonamides, vitamin K, antibiotics; Maintaining hygiene prevents diseases.

Symptoms of coccidiosis: diarrhoea with bloody mucus in it; pink intestinal tissue in droppings; lack of appetite; slow development; anemia; etc...

The treatment is more effective if it's done in the first days of disease. Most of the medications must be added in water. Treatments with sulfonamides will have to be associated with vitamin K3 to prevent hemorrhagic phenomenon caused by sulfaquinoxaline.

Treatments with Amprolium (Thiamine) should last for 5-7 days and they are also known to have a reduced toxicity.

It's also good to administer some polivitamines to your birds.

Maintaining hygiene and proper food prevents diseases.

Ascariasis

Is a parasitic disease caused by parasites (Ascaridia galli), which affects 3-4 months old young birds, turkeys, geese, pigeons, parrots, etc...

Ascaridia galli is a white-yellowish colored worm.

Youngsters can get infected orally through infested water or feed. Massive infestation with worms could lead to the blockage of the intestine causing death if it's not treated in time.

Symptoms of ascariasis: weakness, anorexia, diarrhoea, anaemia, hypovitaminosis, the youngsters stop developing, etc...

Treatments: piperazine salts are effective in treatments against ascariasis. Cambendazole in food for 5 days. Fenbendazole (Panacur) in feed for 4 days. Mebendazol in feed for 7 days. Flubendazole in feed for 7 days. Disinfection of the cage or aviary through flaming and periodical disinfection of the birds is required.

Skin and feather problems

Massive molting represents the slow growth process of feathers. The affected birds have broken and disintegrated feathers.

There are multiple causes like food deficiency (the lack of amino acids, vitamins and minerals), improper maintenance (insufficient light and humidity), liver or kidney disease, tumour or hormonal disorders.

Soft molting it's a permanent or partial feather loss of the bird. The most important causes are high level of humidity, lack of light and food deficiency.

French molting is characterized by the continuous growth and loss of feathers without the possibility to manage to cover all parts of the bird's body. There are a few possible causes that produces the french molt, like viruses (Polyoma or Circoviruses, which have the potential to inflame feather follicles), environment changes, hereditary problems, parasites and nutrition problems. If you notice patches of bare skin on your bird's body or the molting process is not running normally, then you should visit your avian vet as soon as possible.

Inflammation of the skin (Dermatitis)

Inflammation of the skin could appear among other diseases like renal diseases with increasing level of uric acid in the blood, liver disease or infestation with external parasites.

You can use the following therapeutic measures:
- applying astringent and disinfectant solution on the wet wounds. Do not use ointments, because the feathers will become greasy and the bird may peck the wound.
- there are injections with antibiotics which stops the bacterial infestations. Injections with multivitamins and immune system boosters can help the bird to fight against diseases.
- in case that there are itching problems, it would be recommended to use some special anesthetic powder for external use, on the affected areas of the skin. In this case the skin will be anaesthetised and the itchiness should disappear.
- when the bird is scratching too much causing massive bleeding, a collar should be applied around the bird's neck. (In some cases the bird won't be happy to support the collar, especially if the itchiness was caused by physical problems (stress), and maybe this solution (collar) will not resolve the problem)

Xanthomas (Fatty tumors)

Xanthoma is a skin disease which affects overweight birds, especially parrots. Beneath the skin there are deposits of fatty tumors, which have yellowish color and they can be found in chest area, the wing tips, and in ventral and femoral regions (between the legs and around the vent).

These encapsulated benign tumors are composed of mature fat cells. The affected areas can be easily damaged or ulcerated, especially when they grow bigger. Birds will cause self-trauma by pecking them. Xanthoma is a very common disease at birds which are fed exclusively on seeds. You'll need to introduce in the bird's diet some millet, fruits, herbs, green leafy veggies.

Once the bird gets all the necessary food, the existent fatty deposits will stop developing. The eczema should be disinfected with an antiseptic solution.

Reproductive problems

Excessive egg laying

Excessive egg laying in birds can cause calcium deficiency. If we separate the female from the male or remove the nest, will cause stress.

There are several types and sizes of fake or plastic eggs available online or in pet shops. To control egg laying in your pet birds, simply replace the original eggs with plastic eggs. This is a good method that can be applied for the female. When she lays eggs and you don't want to keep the fertile eggs, replace them with the plastic ones and let the female sit her normal period on the plastic eggs. During egg sitting period the female`s body will recover from egg laying.

Egg binding

A frequent problem at cage birds is the retention of the egg. If the hen looks unwell, if she is lethargic and shows signs of an enlarged area around the vent, then her life is in danger.

If the hen can't lay the egg, it could over press the internal organs. The impossibility to eliminate droppings, could lead to self intoxication. It can happen because of the age of the bird (too old), the size and shape of the egg, the sudden drop of temperature 53.6 degrees Fahrenheit (12 degrees Celsius) and the stress during the egg laying process. At the first signs of egg binding, the wet heat will help in most of the cases.

You'll have to place a bowl filled with hot water in front of the cage. The cage must be covered with a towel and the hot steams have to be directed towards the cage. A heating lamp or bulb (60 W) will be necessary near the cage and directed towards the suffering bird. You can also help your bird by introducing 0.5-1 ml of warm oil in the cloacal orifice. This operation should continue each hour until the egg is delivered.

The temperature in the room has to be maintained around 86 degrees Fahrenheit (30 degrees Celsius).

For the bird`s safety, the vet intervention is required.

Aviary plants and shrubs

Here are a few plants and shrubs that will delight your birds, but remember any plant can cause harm if your bird consumes a large enough amount of it.

Blackberry (Rubus fruticosus)

Birch (Betula spp.)

Marigold (Calendula officinalis)

Lemon balm (Melissa officinalis)

Snowberry (Symphoricarpos albus): the birds will find this plant fascinating;

Dog Rose (Rosa canina): it has scarlet hips and beautiful flowers;

Hawthorn (Crataegus monogyna): it is ideal for nesting;

Delphinium: the birds will enjoy the seeds of this plant;

Valerian (Centranthus ruber): can be planted anywhere, the roots have restraint effect on rats;

Sunflower (Helianthus multiflorus): can be planted anywhere;

Tree Mallow (Lavatera olbia): it has red flowers which grow up in July and August;

Holly (Ilex aquifolium): birds will love this plant;

Oregon Grape (Mahonia aquifolium): that shrub will survive most ravages or soils.

Jasmine (Jasminum officinale): there are summer and winter varieties which will produce yellow or white flowers;

Dandelion (Taraxacum officinale): is a very nutritious plant

Plants that can cause intoxication to your parrots

Rhododendron, Flamingo flower (Anthurium), Snowdrop (Galanthus nivalis), Geranium or stork's bills (Pelargonium), Bearberry (Rhamnus purshiana), Ivy (Hedera helix), Lesser celandine (Ranunculus ficaria), Deadly nightshade (Atropa belladonna), Tobacco (Nicotiana tabacum), Mistletoe (Viscum album), Philodendron (Monstera deliciosa), Wood spurge (Euphorbia amygdaloides), Autumn crocus (Colchicum autumnale), Avocado (Persea americana), Peach (Prunus persica), Tomato (Lycopersicon esculentum).

Disclaimer

The author accepts no responsibility for any loss or injury, as a result for the use or misuse of the information in this book.

You should always ask for a qualified advice from your avian vet, before you plan using any medication especially antibiotics. Always check and double check the prescription that should come along with the medication you intend to use for your birds.

I hope this book will help you keep your birds happy and healthy and it is been a pleasure for me to write it down for you.

If you enjoyed the book, will you, please, leave a review? It would be greatly appreciated!

Please check the following page where you can find my other writings:

More from the author

1.Bird Care: Ringneck Parakeets: Diseases and Treatments

2.Bird Care: Keeping Happy And Healthy Ringneck Parakeets

3.Bird Care: Backyard Chickens: Diseases and Treatments

4.Natural Remedies For Men`s Health Problems

5. African Grey Parrots: All About Nutrition, Training, Care, Diseases And Treatments

6. Bird Care African Grey Parrots: Diseases and Treatments

7. Bird Care: Keeping Happy and Healthy Congo African Grey Parrots

8. Zebra Finches: The Complete Guide to Keeping Happy and Healthy Finches

9. Bird Care Zebra Finches: Diseases & Treatments

10. Natural Remedies - How to prevent and cure any diseases with plants from A-Z

11. Citron - Crested Cockatoos: All About Nutrition, Training, Care, Diseases And Treatments

12. Bird Care: Keeping Happy And Healthy Citron - Crested Cockatoos

13. Bird Care: Citron - Crested Cockatoos: Diseases and Treatments

14. Senegal parrots: All About Nutrition, Training, Care, Diseases and Treatments

15. Bird Care: Keeping Happy And Healthy Senegal parrots

16. Bird Care: Senegal Parrots: Diseases and Treatments

17. Cooking for parrots

18. Cockatiels: All About Nutrition, Training, Care, Diseases And Treatments

19. Bird Care: Keeping Healthy And Happy Cockatiels

20. Bird Care: Cockatiels: Diseases and Treatments

21. Lovebirds: All About Nutrition, Training, Care, Diseases and Treatments

22. Bird Care: Keeping Happy And Healthy Lovebirds

23. Bird Care Lovebirds: Diseases And Treatments

24. Natural remedies for Zebra Finches: Herbal Teas

25. Natural remedies for Ringneck Parakeets: Herbal Teas

26. Natural remedies for African Grey parrots: Herbal Teas

27. Natural remedies for Lovebirds: Herbal Teas

28. Natural remedies for Cockatiels: Herbal Teas

You can find all these books on Amazon.com

Brought to you by Erika Busecan

Made in the USA
Middletown, DE
23 July 2019